# "YOUR RIGHTS"
### What Employers Do
### Not Want You to know
#### CDM3Publisher.com

## TABLE OF CONTENTS

### FOR EMPLOYEES ONLY
"Because you have the right to know"

Bibliography end of manuscript

CAROL DENISE MITCHELL

S0-CDN-011

# DEDICATION PAGE

Thanks to workers across America, the outstanding men and women in private, state, local, and federal agencies, often unknown and unseen whose earnest intendments are to serve employers well.

Special thanks to my brother Attorney, Ron Coulter *and to Freta Rogers, for building a great web-site and outstanding cover.*

Thanks to my beloved grandmother, *Garthia Pierson*, my mother, *Tasceaie Charles*, my father, *Zebbie Charles*, and my children Shuun Caldwell and Daryle Thompson and to my fifteen brothers and sisters!

Heartfelt thanks to friends, *Victoria McKinney, Debbie Barwela, Arthur Levy, Attorney at Law, Gary Tavares, Dr. Bowen Wong, Dr. Jed Susseman,* and *Tracision Brown*, whose constant support is valued and appreciated forevermore.

*In memory of Mamus, Mother, Daddy, Zebbie Charles Jr., Victor Newell Charles and Annie Davis, your inspiring lives bring light to my soul. You are missed.*

## "YOUR RIGHTS"
♠♠♠
What Employers Do Not
Want You To Know

AROL

# MITCHELL

## "YOUR RIGHTS
WHAT EMPLOYERS
DO NOT WANT YOU TO KNOW"

ALL RIGHTS RESERVED
**FIRST EDITION**
International Standard Book Number 0-9786258-0-3
CDM3PUBLISHER.COM

◘

## FOR EMPLOYEES ONLY

CDM3
*Writing for
the People
Since 1995*

**CAROL DENISE MITCHELL BOOKS**
**©CDM3 PUBLISHER.COM**
Concord ● California ● United States of America

# "YOUR RIGHTS"
♣♣♣
### What Employers Do Not Want You To Know

This book is a work of non-fiction, but some names, characters, places and incidents are fictional and are products of the author's imagination or are used fictitiously. Any resemblance to actual events/locales or persons, living or dead is entirely coincidental.

CAROL MITCHELL BOOKS
Post Office Box 484, Concord, California 94522 - 0484

Edited by Ron Coulter, Attorney at Law
Supervisory Editor, Carol D. Mitchell
Website: CDM3Publisher.com
First September - 2006

CDM and Carol Denise Mitchell are trademarks of
CDM-3 Publisher - ISBN 0-9786258-0-3

*Author photo: Richard Wallace*
*Cover art & jacket design by: Freta Rogers*
Printed in the United States of America, USA

# "YOUR RIGHTS"
### ♠♠♠
What Employers Do Not
Want You To Know

## From the Publisher

My sincere incentive for writing this guide is to bring into being a much more level playing field for the employee in a rapidly changing and fluid modern working environment. The archetypal American worker goes to work to keep a roof over his/her head and to provide food on the table for their families. When they are hired to work for a company, few employees are told up front about <u>all</u> of their employment rights. Therefore, American workers are truly at the mercy of the employer, who can out wit and outlast the everyday working person. Reality proves that the everyday worker must learn the defenses they are going to need if their earnest work efforts and good intentions on a job go awry. While many employers have fancy law firms defending their interest; employees have few resources to fight back with, and they have even less time to do the research to carry it out. While the employer is fully aware of employment rights and the law, few employees know their rights. That is why I have written this handbook. This guide is specifically for the employee. For it is necessary in this highly technical society to have first hand knowledge of what is needed for one to protect their own interest. Being smart in acquiring the right job means understanding the characteristics and qualifications that employers are looking for in you. A serious job candidate should treat the employment resume like it is the tailor-made suit or gown for their wedding. Fit it to meet distinct body measurements that will display your best attributes directly in calibration with the employer's requirements. When you are hired, be in step with what is going on with the employer. Understand your rights under Department of Labor employment law. Comprehend the many excellent choices you do have in choosing the employer that is right for you. Examine the list in this book of *"100 Best Companies to Work for in America,"* and see if one of the five largest temporary employment agencies listed in this guide is the right employer for you.

With that in mind, I have taken great measures in this book to observe the employer introspectively. I wanted to know why they keep paper trails, and what they do with them. Even more importantly than that, I wanted to know why they fire, how they fire, and how you could work towards keeping the job you love. When I unearthed answers that I felt were right for you, I then harnessed that well-regulated information and the employer's ubiquitous thinking about you from the reverse perspective to give to you, the employee. After reading this chief employee tool-guide, you will have at your fingertips information you will need to be treated fairly on your job.

Additionally, you will be set to get out into the job market professionally knowing what company to work for, and what to say on the interview to nail the job. Then, you will deliver to your employer exactly what is expected of you with precision knowledge, for after you read this guide, you will be informed.

Consequently, if you already have a job, you will have increased certainty in your ability to deliver to your company what your employer wants. Additionally, with your acquired wisdom you will have the ability to fight for your rights. Unfortunately, if it turns out that you have to wage warfare for your job; then you will have the basic tools to cogently wage a fierce and successful battle over whatever may be rightfully yours.

Remember that a good employee and a good employer generally want the same things. The employee wants to know what the company is about and how to become an integral part of the enterprise. The employer wants you to learn what they are about, be a team player, and produce. However, when employees are productive for a company they want to know that their genuine, efforts are appreciated in the workplace. Notwithstanding, the sad reality of this day is that many employees never get praise or the two simple words from their supervisors or managers that can make all the difference in the world towards continual commitment and productivity, and those words are "thank you." While employees are starving for this kind of affirmation from the employer; we live in a litigious society and employers know that some employees are smart enough to write kind gestures and inculpable praises down to use later if things at work go wrong. Consequently, employers are disinclined sometimes to give credit openly where it is due, thereby creating a lack of communication and understanding of the employee's remarkable accomplishments.

Sadly, It does not cost a company a dime to say kind words to individuals who are being productive. Saying, *"hey, just want to tell you to keep up the good work,"* can mean all the difference in the world to the individual who is hardworking and giving.

It is your right to know how to keep abreast of your employer. I encourage you to keep track of everything. My message to the employee is, *"write it down."* After all, you are trustworthy, and you have taken the time to effectively and accurately live up to the expectations of the employer. Imagine that you wanted to be challenged, so you ranked at the top of the scale for setting forth your visions towards the company's ongoing prosperity. Then you were unceremoniously fired. Say you were a victim of redundancy, and the employer told you that the position you molded, and worked so hard in had been discontinued.

# "YOUR RIGHTS"
♠♠♠
What Employers Do Not
Want You To Know


Three weeks later, your friend and former co-worker tells you that a recent college graduate Joe Blow, with less experience and education than you was hired into your old job just days after you were fired. If something like that happens to you _know your rights_[1]. Read this guide and use your good note taking to prove your previous contributions in the job that you lost. Know who to call, and when to call them.

Discern and understand what forms you need to fill out and how to fill them out properly. If you are in a union get immediate assistance. Read on and review a variety of resources, and information that your boss does not want you to know. Be a better employee for the employer, and most importantly be a better one for you!

_"Democracy cannot work unless it is honored in the factory as well as the polling booth; men cannot be truly free in body and in spirit unless their freedom extends into the places where they earn their daily bread."_

**Senator Robert F. Wagner in 1935,**
Upon offering his Bill that was to become
The Nation's Basic Labor Law.

---

[1] If you are forty years of age or older and you were replaced by someone who was younger than forty years of age, you may be a victim of age discrimination and protected under the Age Discrimination Employment Act (ADEA) as well as your State Anti-Discrimination law.

# "YOUR RIGHTS"
♠♠♠
What Employers Do Not
Want You To Know

National Employment Lawyers Association, (NELA) @ http://www.nela.org/home.cfm

♦ NELA is the country's only professional organization that is exclusively comprised of lawyers who represent individual employees in cases involving employment discrimination and other employment-related matters. The headquarters is located in San Francisco, California.

♦ Workplace Fairness at http://www.workplacefairness.org. This is an excellent web-site for **lay** people to learn about their rights as employees and how to save or get their job back.

## *Ten things employers do not want you to know!*

| | |
|---|---|
| ♦ **The law period** | How to easily interpret difficult contracts/policy |
| ♦ **Where to go for help** | How to acquire immediate help resources to defend your interest |
| ♦ **The Paper Trail** | How they are tracking your *every* effort on the job |
| ♦ **The truth about the "Offer Letter"** | How it is a *legal and binding* contract of employment |
| ♦ **Title VII of the Civil Rights Act** | How it protects you against harassment, discrimination, etc. |
| ♦ **Age Discrimination, (ADEA)** | How you can fight after being fired over 40 |
| ♦ **Who is in Charge** | How to contact *decision making executives* for resolve |
| ♦ **Workers Compensation Law** | They particularly do not want their insurance rates to go up |
| ♦ **How to fight for your rights** | For employers; the less you know about your rights, the better |

# "YOUR RIGHTS"
♠♠♠
What Employers Do Not
Want You To Know

## THE DISCLAIMER

The use of this guide is for readers who want easy access to personal and published information regarding employment rights. As more fully set forth in the terms of your using this guide, the data provided here is for general information purposes; it is not a determination of your legal rights nor your responsibilities under the law. I am not a lawyer, and none of the information contained in this guide is, or should be defined as, legal advice. I am not engaged in the practice of law, and no attorney-client relationship is being created. Any information communicated to any lawyer via this guide does not have the confidentiality protection of the attorney/client privilege. Laws do change often. This guide contains information that is current to date and the purpose of this guide is to provide you with information that will be illuminative. If you are seeking legal advice, find a qualified lawyer in your area. If you need help in finding a lawyer, call your local, county, state bar association, or check out the information below.

♦   National Employment Lawyers Association, (NELA) @ http://www.nela.org/home.cfmNELA is the largest and most effective plaintiff employment lawyer organization in the United States. The headquarters is located in San Francisco, California.

♦   Workplace Fairness at Http://www.workplacefairness.org. This is an excellent web-site for _lay_ people to learn about their rights as employees and how to save or get their job back

# "YOUR RIGHTS"
♠♠♠
What Employers Do Not
Want You To Know

## What Is An Employee

Before I explain to you the many ways in which you can defend your employment rights, you must first know what the word employee means to you. Generally, the definition of the word, "employee" has varying meanings. However, when it comes to you knowing what role "employee" in a company is, be aware that you are an employee if a company hires you to perform a distinct form of labor or work. Your offering to a specific job or industry has a lot to do with what job you were hired to do, and how your skills, and or education and experience match, and can positively influence ongoing residual profit for the company. Work titles cover a wide range of professional business from accountants to lawyers. With the recent boom in technology, some professional work titles are transcending conventional definition and are changing with trends. Some employees, *(depending on the work contract),* are permanent and they receive a guaranteed wage. Others may be hired as temporary employees, contract employees, or as consultants. Self-employed employees who own entire businesses are usually in trade for themselves; however, if they have just a person working for them they may be considered an employee of the client for tax purposes.

## WHAT IS EMPLOYMENT

Employment is a contract and or grouping between two parties, the *employer* and the *employee*. The employee is typically chosen via a competitive hiring process where other candidates are eliminated. This process may include but is not limited to:

♦ Filling out an employment application

♦ Interviewing with the hiring manager and or supervisor of the department

♦ Second, & sometimes third interviews with management level professionals

When hired the employee signs on with the employer. The newly hired person then services the employer in a mercantile setting giving suitable and congruous productivity to the hiring party with the intention of maintaining and or creating profits. The hired employee works in public, nonprofit and or private settings and then dispenses labor to the hiring entity or enterprise in return for a pre-specified amount of pay or wages. In the United States most employees are designated "at will." In this case, either the employer or employee can *(without fear of reprisal)* stop employment, at any time for any cause or simply for no reason.

# "YOUR RIGHTS"
♠♠♠
What Employers Do Not
Want You To Know

**Note:**   **From the US Department of Labor**

The total number of US technical jobs is around 8.5 million

3.3 million jobs are expected to be offshore out-sourced to India and China

Over the next several years. (2003 Business Week)

# "YOUR RIGHTS"
♠♠♠
What Employers Do Not
Want You To Know

◘

*CHAPTER 1*

### Getting off to the Right Start

**The most important thing to take to work each day is**

1.     The *Smart Page Weekly hand-sheet*. In time of need - it will be your guiding light.

Write something on your sheet or diary everyday. If you take public transportation to work, instead of reading the paper, write down events of the previous day. You will be glad at how useful this information can be. Even the most mundane and unimportant things today, could be your saving grace tomorrow!

**Five reasons why it is important to write things down**

1.    It's hard to lie about an exact date and or time

2.    Pinning times and dates give you more credibility

3.    Your memory can not always be relied upon

4.    Facts can be sustained easier

5.    It jogs your memory better

**Help is on the way!**

The employer is on your trail. Therefore, your Smart Page Weekly hand-sheet allows you to record your good work and write down areas where you want to grow and keep track of all of your special projects and your overtime hours in a neat way that you will invariably need later. With smart tips, handy charts, snappy letters, resumes and much more, this useful data guide, will spare you the overall trouble of worrying where to go to handle your business when it comes to your job and how to produce important facts. With your great attention to detail, save your job, and prove to your employer exactly how well you really have been doing it. Know how important government work web-sites will be if you need to file a claim for unemployment insurance, or whatever you need in your employment future. Check out your Smart Page Weekly hand-sheet below and download other forms easily using information provided for you at the following government links!

# "YOUR RIGHTS"
♠♠♠
What Employers Do Not
Want You To Know

- U.S. Department of Labor, www.dol.gov

- U.S. Equal Employment Opportunity Commission www.eeoc.gov

- U.S. Department of Justice, www.usdoj.gov

- The Internal Revenue Service, www.irs.gov

Being able to access important help pages will save you the time of wondering where to go for information and where to get important forms. Many web pages allow you to download forms easily. Did you know that you can apply for Unemployment benefits on line? In California, there are few places, if any to go fill out unemployment forms. Now it's easier to download forms on the computer. Go online even, and complete an application that is processed more expeditiously! Even if your job is not threatened today, each employee should know what's out there for him or her in case they have to use these resources tomorrow. No employee can ever have too much information when it comes to implementing and exercising employment rights.

## Smart Page Weekly Hand-sheet ▶▶▶▶▶▶ ▶▶▶▶▶▶

| | FIRST: | LAST: |
|---|---|---|
| Name Here | | |
| Address Here | | |
| Telephone Here | | City/State/Zip |
| Cell/Mobile Here | | |
| E-mail/Website Here | | |

| Employment Information | Smile Notes | PLACE OF EMPLOYMENT |
|---|---|---|
| | | COMPANY NAME |
| Start Date\ | | COMPANY ADDRESS |
| Position Title\ | | COMPANY PHONE |

| Weekly Work Track Record | | | | | | Weekly Hand-sheet Work Comments |
|---|---|---|---|---|---|---|
| Monday | Date: | Y= OK | N=Not | Y | N | |
| Tuesday | Date: | Y= OK | N=Not | Y | N | |
| Wednesday | Date: | Y= OK | N=Not | Y | N | |
| Thursday | Date: | Y= OK | N=Not | Y | N | |
| Friday | Date: | Y= OK | N=Not | Y | N | |
| Saturday | Date: | Y= OK | N=Not | Y | N | |
| Sunday | Date: | Y= OK | N=Not | Y | N | |

| Project Day | Project Name | Happy Notes | Detailed Comments |
|---|---|---|---|
| 1. Monday | | | |
| 2. Tuesday | | | |
| 3. Wednesday | | | |
| 4. Thursday | | | |
| 5. Friday | | | |

| Overtime worked, explain in comments Name of project worked on: | More comments on overtime: |
|---|---|
| Amount of time: _____ | Approved by: _____  Date approved: _____ |
| Amount of time: _____ | Approved by: _____  Date approved: _____ |
| Amount of time: _____ | Approved by: _____  Date approved: _____ |

☐ **Reminder**: Copy for quick reference to preserve memorable work facts.

## MY Smart Page Weekly WORKSHEET

**Employee Name** _____

**Title:** _____    **Date:** _____

| Date/In/Out to be checked ⅂ | | | | Daily Time | Hourly report. Hours worked, and recorded for personal records. |
|---|---|---|---|---|---|
| reaks | In | Out | Lunchtime | | COMMENTS |
| | | | | 8:00 | |
| | | | | 9:00 | |
| | | | | 10.00 | |
| | | | | 11:00 | |
| | | | | 12:00 | |
| | | | | 1:00 | |
| | | | | 2:00 | |
| | | | | 3:00 | |
| | | | | 4:00 | |
| | | | | 5:00 | |
| | | | | | ---------- **Daily Work & Time Report**---------- |

Employee's signature    Week ending date

# "YOUR RIGHTS"
### ♠♠♠
What Employers Do Not
Want You To Know

### Smart Employee Preparation Tool

## The professional you

By now you know that if the employer threatens your livelihood - you are going to wage a battle for your rights. Before then, in order to ensure that you are on the right footing with the employer, you must be serious about doing your part fully when it comes to your job.

At work, be courteous, be polite, be considerate, be concerned, be respectful, and be quietly professional at all times. Give the employer a chance to be good to you!

| | |
|---|---|
| ☐ Don't be the company clown | ► Do buy a thesaurus; use it! |
| ☐ Don't get drunk at work, or luncheons | ► Do finish projects completely |
| ☐ Don't give gifts to the boss | ► Do influence others positively |
| ☐ Don't *clown* the boss in public | ► Do offer solutions to problems |
| ☐ Don't address anyone as, "hey you" | ► Do think, then speak |
| ☐ Don't lose your strong work ethic | ► Do exercise savvy Internet skills |
| ☐ Don't ever be late for work | ► Do the nice thing to all |

## On our honor, we do our duty

Most employees arrive to work ready to give 100% to the employer, as they should. As good workers, we honor the employer by giving our complete dedication, our promised dependability and full obligation to carry out our job in the way that we are hired for. Many of us are not college graduates and some of us are. The majority of us have a commendable work ethic. We come to work eager and prepared to do the job.

We ask the right questions in turn we receive the right answers towards a long future with a great company. When things don't turn out right at work, there are many factors to be considered other than that I am not doing my job. Unfortunately, many employees who go to work to serve are often victimized, or cheated when things at work go awry. Employees in general have little time to endure a long process of fighting for benefits, lost wages or other compensation that are due to them when the work relationship dies. Therefore, employees will march off the job leaving behind earned overtime payments, worker's compensation benefits, unemployment insurance benefits and unresolved discrimination and harassment claims.

# "YOUR RIGHTS"
♠♠♠
## What Employers Do Not
## Want You To Know

While you are fed up, your employer is aware that laws are ever changing. Your well-informed employer is therefore keeping your money in the bank. They are drawing interest on your funds banking that you will move on with your life, rather than claim from them what is rightfully yours. Moreover, behind your back, the employer has an impressive paper trail on you. So, why not start-off with the Company by giving the employer exactly what they are looking for.

### Know what they want

According to surveys, employers seek the following qualifications in recent college graduates. This list can serve as a guide for those who want to sell themselves for what employers say they want.

| Work Experience | Computer Work | Problem Solving Skills |
|---|---|---|
| If you are applying for a job as a receptionist, you may have had some skills in your early past that helps you build experience for that job. For instance, if you worked in your high-school administrative office, use that towards experience on your application to be a receptionist. | With the increased demand for IT professionals and jobs alike, computer experience is required for just about every job in business, education and government agencies. If you have a computer at home and you make flyers, or write down notes; use that experience on your job application. | When the employer is trying to ascertain your level of critical thinking, use clear and concise situations where your problem solving skills has tangibly offset what could have been a worse problem. Personal life experiences can help you build a resume in line with what the employer is looking for! |

### Did you know?

It is your right to:

- Refuse to work seven days straight (*unless your employer is exempt by law?*)

- Vote. Tip: (*Always give your employer notice.*) It is your right to vote!

- Take time off work to appear as a witness. Tip: (*Give your employer notice.*)

- Serve on a jury. (Yes, give *them* notice.)

# "YOUR RIGHTS"
♠♠♠
### What Employers Do Not
### Want You To Know

- File for bankruptcy and not be fired!

Intentional or not, many supervisors, and or managers are not fully aware how to make sure that all of your rights are protected and that includes hiring without illegal discrimination. Therefore, it is up to you, the employee, to embrace the laws that protect you in the interview, and then in the workplace. Be ready, be equipped and be smart when it comes to your employment rights.

| Communication Skills | Leadership Experiences | Dependability |
|---|---|---|
| In the professional work environment, nothing says it more than a person who speaks well and gets along well with people from diverse, and all cultures. Use your strong writing, research and public speaking experience to clarify on your application your strong communication skills. | Many of us have participated in activities that have honed our developmental and social skills, and we discount them because we feel that they are not job related. Consider using all applicable skills for the job, you are interested in applying. | Whether you are a college graduate or not, you probably know how important it is to show up on a job everyday at the right time. Prove to your employer that you know the importance of being a dependable employee that they can rely on to be on time and at work everyday. |

## Winning points to remember:

Use all relevant work and life skills towards getting the job

Never, ever lie on your application or job resume

Know your strengths and weaknesses

In interviews, downplay weak points, play up strengths

Be positive. Speak well of others; be a problem solver

Never, ever be late for work: (leave earlier to get there on time)

# "YOUR RIGHTS"
♠♠♠
What Employers Do Not
Want You To Know

◘

CHAPTER 2
## Employee in the Know

### From the beginning

When you seek out a company for employment, you are asking them to entrust you to be a part of an industry that many companies consider family. If you are hired, you are going to be at the business more than one quarter of the day. You are the greatest resource of the business because with your skills, work experience and education, you are valuable. The employer knows that managing people correctly can take up priceless production time. Therefore, to keep controversy to a minimum, the lawyers have given employers an employee blueprint on how to effectively hire and fire you. Beware!

They are going to give you a ***Job Description***. They are going to imply, but not tell you that the job description clarifies your role <u>fully</u>. They use the job description to avoid mystification about your role, define the essential functions of the position, and to have a leg to stand on legally if you sue them later.

They are going to provide you with a document generally termed an "***Employment Offer" or "Offer of Employment"***. This letter is designed with more structure than the Golden Gate Bridge. Lawyers advise companies to give you this letter before you start the job. They want you to read the letter and sign it. Once you have signed the employment letter and returned it to the employer, you have officially signed a *legal contract*, which in most cases will be careful not to provide you with a property interest in the position. If the employer does not tell you that there is a probationary period in the letter, they may have negated an important key regarding your employment rights.

The ***Probationary period*** can be used as a tool to summarily fire you at anytime during the specified time of probation. A usual feature of a probationary period is that the employer may end your employment without affording you a due process procedure that may be afforded to non-probationary employees. Usually a probationary period is ninety days. In most companies, employee's legal status is at will. Simply put, "at will" employees may be terminated for any legal reason at the discretion of the employer. The employer may fire the employee for anything or the employee may leave for any reason without giving notice to the employer.

However, to play it smart, they may simply fire you without cause saying that you did not pass the probationary period and unless they have violated your ***protected rights***, there is little you can do about an "at will" firing. Generally a private sector employee, who is not carried by a union, is considered to be "at will" under the law.

Therefore, without a written employment contract, or prevailing enforceable verbal contract, an employer may without breaking the laws per se, fire an employee, so long as they do not breach a protected class or break the law. ***Remember:*** it is always wise to do your research, using the resources provided herein, and challenge an employer who fires you for no reason.

Judges are keenly aware of the "at will" laws. They know the law allows employers to fire innocent people sometimes. Again, for probation to be sensible, and adequate, it has to be agreed upon between yourself and the employer before you start the job.

***References.*** **Employment Defense** Lawyers and other employer advocates believe that there are an increasing number of people providing false employment details and fake references to promote their bid for the job. ***TIP:*** They are telling the employer to confirm your references and to talk directly to past employers or they will use professional screening services to track down the truth. ***Advice:*** Be honest. Even if you had a bad relationship with a past employer, call them. Ask them to give you a start, and end date, of your last job on company letterhead. Tell them it is against the law to tell a future employer things about you that are not true. That way when you fill out an application for a new job, you have tangible proof from the Department of Human Resources that your dates are accurate. No company wants to risk a potential defamation lawsuit. Instead, your former company will be more than willing to give you a start and end date reference. You cannot always rely on friends or false references.

**Employment Defense** Lawyers and other employer advocates are telling the employer to settle. If the employer has not done things right by you from the beginning, they dig themselves a hole. Let me be honest. There are unqualified people wearing big hats in companies that do not know how to be fair to employees. Unprofessional behavior and incompetence on the part of the employer can cost time and money regardless whether the company at issue is right or wrong.

# "YOUR RIGHTS"
♠♠♠
## What Employers Do Not
## Want You To Know

Good and fair employment practices are vital to a serious business. Good employment practice can reduce cost. Therefore, you can help your company maintain being a great employer by assuring yourself of the following:

- Follow the company rules

- Know your legal employee/employment rights

- Keep your own paper trail to match or better employer

- Stay calm, resolve work issues, try not to get fired

- Call your lawyer to read employment agreements, contracts

**Special note regarding your pension & important U.S. Department of Labor facts**

If you have been with a company for a long time and they owe you a pension, check into it religiously. You are entitled to your pension. You earned this money through your dedicated service and if something is not right with your pension, then you should contact the U.S. Department of Labor's Pension and Welfare Benefit Administration (PWBA), for assistance at http://www.dol.gov/dol/topic/retirement/participantrights.htm

Your earnings are important to you. Did you know that the U.S. Department of Labor compiles Labor Statistics Data to keep assiduous track of your hours? Your employer takes keeping track of your hours seriously enough to provide this data (regularly) to the government. Below, see one example of who is working overtime and why you must keep track of _**your own personal time**_ as attentively as they keep track of you!

From U.S. Department of Labor Bureau of Labor Statistics - www.bls.gov

Employment, Hours and Earnings from the Current Employment Statistics Survey (National)

| | | |
|---|---|---|
| **Series ID:** | *CES0100000005* | |
| **Seasonally Adjusted** | Super Sector: | NATURAL RESOURCES AND MINING |
| **NAICS Code**: | N/A    Data Type: | AVG WEEKLY HOURS OF PRODUCTION WORKERS |
| **FACTS:** | The average US production worker put in more than five hours of overtime consistently from January 2005 - July 2005. In July alone, the average weekly hours put in by American production workers averaged 45.7 hours per week. | |

# "YOUR RIGHTS"
♠♠♠
What Employers Do Not
Want You To Know

Knowing Your Time-Card
## SAMPLE COMPANY TIME-CARD

After reviewing the data above, it is consequential for you to keep track of all hours worked, regular and overtime. Audit and store all of your work check stubs. Double check regular time, training time for a new job, overtime and determine if double-time is recorded correctly on ***EACH*** time card record. Make sure your deductions are correct. Add and subtract your totals to make sure you are being paid accurately for all time worked. Review the sample check stub below. Practice your math, until you are confident that you understand your check stub. Under California Labor Code §§ 226-226.6; Industrial Relations your check should contain the following information:

- Gross wages earned

- Total amount of hours worked

- All Deductions

- Net wages earned

- Date you were paid for including: month, day and year

- Social Security number

- Name and Address of the employer

- Number of piece rates units earned

- Hourly rate of pay

# "YOUR RIGHTS"
♠♠♠
What Employers Do Not
Want You To Know

| W STARTS SOFTWARE COMPANY | | Check No. | 48998 |
| 11 W. IMPERIAL HIGHWAY | | Check Date: | 05/16/2005 |
| ITE # 111 | | Period Ending: | 05/30/2005 |
| REA, CA 92821 | | Pay Frequency: | BI-Weekly |

| E, JANE E. | ID NUMBER: 50104 | STATUS | EXEMPT | TAX ADJUSTMENTS | STATE AND LOCAL CODES |
|---|---|---|---|---|---|
| 5 Greater Street - Apartment #16 | BASE RATE: 30.00 | FED: SINGLE | 02 | FED: | PRI: CA LOC1: LOC3: |
| 1 Francisco, CA 94110 | SSN: 566-00-XXXX | ST1: S | 02 | STATE | SEC: LOC2: LOC4: |
| | | ST2: | | DI/UC: | LOC5: |
| | | | | LOCAL | |

## IMPORTANT MESSAGE

| HOURS AND EARNINGS | TAXES AND DEDUCTIONS | SPECIAL INFORMATION |
|---|---|---|

| CURRENT | | | DESCRIPTION | | CURRENT AMOUNT | |
|---|---|---|---|---|---|---|
| DESCRIPTION | HOURS/UNIT | EARNINGS | | SOCIAL SECURITY | 29.88 | |
| REGULAR | 26.0 | 286.00 | | MEDICARE | 6.99 | |
| TRAINING | 16.0 | 108.00 | | | | |
| OVERTIME | 4.0 | 66.00 | | SDI/UC | 4.34 | |
| DOUBLETIME | 1.0 | 22.00 | | | | |
| | | | | TOTAL | 41.21 | |
| | | | | | | |
| | | | | AFTER-TAX DEDUCTIONS | | |
| TOTAL H/E | 47.0 | 482.00 | | | | |

| PRE-TAX ITEMS | | | | | | |
|---|---|---|---|---|---|---|
| OTAL | 482 | | | | | |
| | EARNINGS | PRETAX | FIT TAXABLE | LESS TAXES | LESS DEDS | EQ NET PAY |
| CURRENT | 482.00 | 0.00 | 482.00 | 41.21 | 0.00 | **440.79** |

STATEMENT OF EARNINGS, DETACH AND KEEP FOR YOUR RECORDS

## Important payroll tip(s)

Never call payroll acting a fool because you were shorted money on your paycheck. Humans are not perfect.

Moreover, we are all inclined to make errors sometimes. Never use profanity. It is not cool. A mad or pissed-off

payroll clerk can find ways to delay you not getting your money. Be smart, at the same time, be serious, and be

professional.

1.     Find out who the payroll clerk is. Next, e-mail her a precise, (short) message regarding money you were

        not paid.

2.     Copy your check stub, and offer to show it to her for review.

3.     Copy your sign-in sheet for the payroll clerk. Be nice.

## CHAPTER 3
### Smoke before the Fire

**Fifteen *possible* reasons why employers will fire you.**

| | | | | | |
|---|---|---|---|---|---|
| ☐ | Insubordination | ☐ | Lying on the application | ☐ | Excessive lateness/absence |
| ☐ | Low productivity | ☐ | Incompetence | ☐ | Negligence |
| ☐ | Sleeping on the job | ☐ | Violation of safety rules | ☐ | Harassment |
| ☐ | Conviction of crime | ☐ | Continual ineptitude | ☐ | Gambling |
| ☐ | Stealing | ☐ | Fighting | ☐ | Use of alcohol/drugs |

☐ **Tell somebody**. To stay on top of your job avoid putting yourself in the line of fire. If you find that your regular work hours are not going to work for you, ask the Company for flex time. Explain to them briefly verbally, and in writing why you need to change your hours. And then, if you are going to be late, call your supervisor, then copy the message to your voice mail to prove that you made the call regarding your lateness. Never take it upon yourself to just come to work late without telling someone.

☐ **Be honest**. Tell the truth on your application. If this is the right job for you, and everything is going well, if you lied on your application it will without fail come back to bite you when you least expect it. If you do not do anything else in this guide, do not lie on your application. Well-documented cases of employees who have lied on their application reveals that many flourished for years in their positions until they were found out. Regardless of all the fortuitous years these employees gave to the Company, once the lie was revealed, they were fired.

### The employer's secret weapon

The Paper Trail is their secret weapon and keeping track of you can be their savanna. Fear not, because the paper trail can work for you as well. They maintain the practices of keeping track of you to build an unassailable defense against you in court and to establish a cause and effect equation that you engaged in prohibited behavior causing them to fire you. Keep that in mind, when you use your personalized hand-sheet to give you a winning advantage on your job. Do your job. Never give your employer a reason to hound your every move.

# "YOUR RIGHTS"
♣♣♣
## What Employers Do Not
## Want You To Know

### Employee access to personnel records

Your personnel records are the property of the employer. Check state law because federal law does not require the employer to give employees access to their personnel file. If you are a federal employee and have an issue regarding your rights and obligations of union, management and employees in a federal workplace represented by a labor union, contact the **Federal Labor Relations Authority** (FLRA) at http://www.flra.gov/. For other employees, all files should only contain job-related information, documentation. At least twenty states including California, Illinois and Massachusetts do let employees into their files. Ask to see the contents of your personnel file regularly in writing, at least twice a year. Be prepared to make copies of this file and literally defend anything in that file that is unfamiliar and outlandish to you.

**Inside tip:** Employers may not want you to have your file if the information in the file will be used to support a legal claim against the Company. Keep your own records to match whatever grievances or conflict your employer may try to boast against you. Ask for copies of everything. If your name is on it, get a copy. Preserve it. If the information contained on work documents is not true or correct, dispute it immediately, *(in writing)*. **_Remember:_** when you are in a fight against your employer, generally, the burden of proof lies with the employer. If your personal work records are as meticulous and straight as theirs are, you have an increased chance of winning your rightful claim against the employer. When the employer discovers that you know your rights, chances are they will not ride you so hard on the small things. Then, you will have time to go on and be the great employee that you are!

### What *they* keep track of

- Your mistakes
- Your conflicts
- Your complaints
- Your work performance

# "YOUR RIGHTS"
## ♠♠♠
### What Employers Do Not
### Want You To Know

## What _you_ keep track of

◎ Your mistakes

◎ Your conflicts

◎ Your complaints

◎ Your work performance

◎ Specific times dates

◎ Witnesses (willing or unwilling)

When you get your performance appraisal, look for the comment(s) section. No matter how small the comments box is, write the correct version of your performance appraisal from your own point of view and then ask co-workers to rate your performance and send them to you in an inter-office email. Take the good e-mails home and store them in a safe place. When it is time for you to advance towards a higher position, produce your positive ratings from co-workers and give them to your supervisor as leverage in getting that higher paying position. **Note**: It is okay to add pages to your performance appraisal. Give yourself a chance to better clarify your duties in a manner that your employer was not perhaps aware.

## If you are being fired, make them do it the right way!

Never _voluntarily quit_ your job and lose dollars due to you under unemployment insurance. If you simply do not want to be fired, _(and you have another job lined up,)_ then quitting would be a practicable option. In any case, if you are going to stick it out make sure the following things are in play before your employment with your job is terminated.

1.  Make sure your employer has given you a fair chance to improve and prove to you in writing that you knew your job was at risk before the termination ensued.

2.  Make sure the employer did not breach your employment contract.

3.  Make sure the employer did not act intentionally to breach your contract.

4.  Make sure the employer follows all federal laws regarding your final paycheck. It is California law to give you the final check immediately upon dismissal. _(This rule may not apply to other states.)_

5.  Ask for severance pay and or all benefits due to you including stock options.

# "YOUR RIGHTS"
♠♠♠
## What Employers Do Not
## Want You To Know

6.  Ask for a *positive* letter of recommendation from the Department of Human Resources, even if you do not think that you deserve it. In a mutual separation from a job, you have more bargaining power than you realize. **Reminder**: during the separation process preserve your dignity be cool, never fight, act crazy or threaten employees or employment staff, or anyone that let you go. Think ahead! Put forth confidence in your closing actions; present a professional demeanor, and then prepare to just move right on to a better job! To vent read on and fill out a *job death certificate*. Frame it as your healthy reminder that when the job dies; I live and I can move on.

7.  Apply for unemployment insurance the next working day that you are let go regardless if you are fired. If you lose unemployment benefits, you may win back wages in the California Unemployment Insurance appeals process.

8.  *AB2690*

    Wages

    All workers employed on public works must be paid the general prevailing rate, except for public works projects of $1,000 or less.

9.  This bill exempts a volunteer, a volunteer coordinator, or members of the California Conservation Corps or certified Community Conservation Corps and goes into effect immediately. The exemption applies retroactively to work concluded on or after January 1, 2002, and continues until January 1, 2009, unless a subsequent law modifies that date. *AB1845* NEW LAW: Unemployment Insurance extends employment retraining benefits for eligible individuals receiving unemployment compensation until January 1, 2010.

    **Tips**: If you get a sympathetic administrative law judge, who values your smart diary information, that clears up disparity in your employer's overall reason's for letting you go; there is a good chance that the administrative law judge will give you the benefit of the doubt over your employer and you will win your benefits. Be honest, be confident, and be prepared when going before a judge.

# "YOUR RIGHTS"
### ♠♠♠
## What Employers Do Not
## Want You To Know

**Here is why!**

Natalie Peeks actually got chills one time when all of her diligence and hard work paid off when a state official took out her ninety-nine cents calculator to visually show the employer how she had been cheated out of overtime pay.

I was happy for Natalie that at the end of that case that she had not given up and that she not only had successfully protected my her overtime interest/rights; but also the rights of others that had been cheated out of overtime by this company. In this case, the official told the employer to straighten up their act, or be prepared to suffer the consequences of a company wide audit. It felt good to sit back with Natalie, who came prepared with her organized notebook and dozens of hand-sheets, and see her not have to say a word in her defense. The sympathetic side of Natalie wanted to bolt to the defense of the HR person. After all, *"even bad companies deserve a little slack after a hearing like that!"* Natalie said! Natalie thought about it a minute, then she shrugged her shoulders and simply decided, "maybe not". In the end, the company called Natalie to thank her for claiming her rights and exposing the deficiencies of their payroll department. That HR person gave Natalie a check for overtime totaling $7,000.00 and the CEO of the company thanked Natalie personally because all employees would benefit from the actions of this brave woman who simply exercised her employment wage rights.

**FYI - Labor Interest/New Law**

Few people know that *The California Unemployment Board of Appeals*, *The Department of Labor,* and other state/government entities are waiting to help you, (*the cheated employee*). New laws are always being implemented towards preserving your being treated fair on the job. New Law: 2004 sharing *penalties SB 1809 has changed the sharing of any penalty that is recovered as a result of an employee lawsuit. Previously any penalty was split 50% to the General Fund, 25% to the Agency and 25% to the employee. Now 75% goes to the Agency specifically designated for enforcement and education of employers and employees of their rights and obligations under the Labor Code. The remaining 25% still go to the employee along with attorney's fees.*
State workers can be overworked and underpaid and in many offices, they do not have the special updated equipment or amenities that are abundant in private industry. When you go to state agencies to get forms always be nice to them and know what forms you need.

# "YOUR RIGHTS"
♠♠♠
### What Employers Do Not
### Want You To Know

You have to bring your hand-sheet or diary, your charts, and your witnesses, most important of all, you must always come with the truth, *and nothing but the truth* so help you God.

### FYI - Smart tip:

If you ever watch *Judge Joe Brown* or *Judge Judy* on television, they will tell you to "chill out" when you are ahead. The same goes for other legal venues.

When you are winning, "don't say a word." Be **quiet** and listen to the judge telling your company off for forty minutes and you will automatically grow a new skin from all of the pain your employer put you through. Sit back at the governing table in your state issued gummy brown wrought iron chair. Draw a deep breath, relax and enjoy the idea that your super power employer has shortly, lost control. Luxuriate in the fact that the company you had battled with for a year over a measly $550.00 in overtime payments, is about to pay you. Finally, pat yourself on the back for riding *your green rights* wagon up to the Board of Directors and then to the Department of Labor. Congratulations! Finally, you are about to win!

### Big brother wants employers to get their *ACT* together

When *The Department of Labor Board* uncovers illegal pay practices in companies, they do not like it. The *National Labor Relations Board,* (NLRB) is designed to conduct investigations and hold hearings involving allegations of unfair labor practices. The NLRB holds and conducts union representation elections, and these elections may involve the certification or de-certification of a union as a bargaining representative of a group of employees and all of this is and was done to preserve your rights.

Employers can not interfere with unionization; management cannot threaten employees, who engage in organizational activities; or take steps designed to erode employees' support for a union and management cannot make persuasive statements during the pre-election discussion of a union's merits.

The Department of Labor has a lot of power, and by the time, you need them, they will be fair. The next time someone tells you to get your act together, consider four (4) very important facts you can shoot back at them:

**Norris-LaGuardia Act:**      This act, which was passed in 1932, restricts federal courts from issuing injunctions to prevent legal union activities. State courts are not restricted in a similar manner.

# "YOUR RIGHTS"
♠♠♠
What Employers Do Not
Want You To Know

| | |
|---|---|
| **Wagner Act:** | Passed in 1935, this law is formally known as the National Labor Relations Act. This act formally recognized the employee's right to organize and participate in union activities. The Wagner Act created the National Labor Relations Board and established five unfair labor practices by management. |
| **Taft-Hartley Act:** | This amendment to the Wagner Act was adopted in 1947. It was designed to adjust the bargaining process, which Congress perceived as favoring the unions. Among its important provisions, the *Taft-Hartley Act* provided an 80-day cooling-off period, outlawed the closed shop contract, allowed employers to have free speech, and created the Federal Mediation and Conciliation Service. As a step to balancing the bargaining process, this act also included unfair labor practices by unions. |
| **Landrum-Griffin Act:** | This also is, an amendment to the Wagner Act. It was passed in 1959. The major purpose of this act is to remove corruption from the internal government of unions and to ensure each union's members a specific bill of rights. |

Never allow the intimidation factor by anyone to stop you from pursuing your employment rights. Where self-doubt and ambiguity lingers, consult with an employment attorney for sound legal advice! You may have a fantastic chance to recover losses from a variety of employment issues, and a legal pro will be all too willing to make those claims for you!

### Getting in the groove for your rights!

It takes patience to fight hard, but you need to know that if you wait for what is due to you, you go to bed feeling happy when you win and you know you are right. Do not second-guess your feelings. If you are going to be leaving a job that hurt you, do not give up. File your paper work with **Small Claims** court, or **The Department of Fair Employment & Housing,** or **The Department of Labor**. It will be a few weeks before your hearing. Never give up. Fight with the truth. File all the right papers and wait for your hearing or court date with patience. Lies are bad. Unfortunately, the opposing side will lie sometimes. Just be prepared. Deal with your case honestly, then if anyone ever tries to take that from you, you fight like hell to defend your good honor.

# "YOUR RIGHTS"
♠♠♠
### What Employers Do Not
### Want You To Know

Then, even if you lose, you win. You only lose when you *do not exercise your rights at all*. Many laws have been put into play for your protection and the governing professionals know when somebody is lying. You need to wear armor of protection and zealously defend your interest. You need to know how to deal with pressure and not let it stop you from defending and getting what is rightfully yours. **Remember:** Rome really was not built in one day, and neither will be your victory!

## Use it or we lose it!

Special agencies put a lot of work into protecting your employment rights. If you do not use these rights, we may lose them. That would be sad for the little people, like you and me and the regular every day worker.

With that in mind, I will address the secrets that you did not know about government agencies.

- State and government agencies can be your best friend

- State and government agencies have little patience for the *lazy employer*

- Be prepared. The government and state agencies can be your champion.

**NOTE:** People that work for the state and the government know the essential value of the word holiday. Generally, private industry workers enjoy fewer holidays than state or government workers do and, they do not care about "all" holidays as do the state, and government agencies.

### Make sure your job complies with employment law

From day one on a new job, look for the colorful, ***"Required Posters for the Workplace."*** Search for the posters in the kitchen or the copy room, and familiarize yourself with the Occupational Safety and Health Administration (OSHA) laws, workers compensation, Equal Employment Opportunity Commission, EEOC and the Department of Fair Employment and Housing, DFEH[2] laws. *(See posters ahead).* Learn who the company doctor is on the OSHA posters in case you get hurt on the job and look for the treatment facilities address and telephone number.

## REFORMED LAW

### Note: Research and apply all new material, provisions to current year's law

The newly reformed law went into effect August 12, 2004. Two provisions apply retroactively to

---

[2] DFEH is the Department of Fair Employment and Housing, a California Fair Employment Practices Agency or FEPA. Most states have such agencies whose functions are to enforce federal as well as state anti-discrimination statutes and other provisions of state or federal law.

# "YOUR RIGHTS"

♠♠♠

What Employers Do Not
Want You To Know

January 1, 2004: Lawsuits for most violations of posting, notice, agency reporting or filing requirements are now excluded from the onerous penalties and private enforcement, except those relating to mandatory payroll or workplace injury reporting; and a court must review and approve penalties in connection with any settlement agreement. *FYI* : *(Remember to always check for current updates on law related subjects.)*

**Remember:**     You have the right to complain to the Occupational Safety and Health Administration, OSHA about safety and health concerns without being penalized for doing so by your employer.

The employee may file a lawsuit if:

> Violations of Labor Code Division 5, which regulates occupational health and safety, except sections 6310, 6311 and 6399.7 requires that before filing a lawsuit, an employee must notify the employer and the Division of Occupational Safety and Health (DOSH), and copy the Agency.
>
> If your work place is unsafe, in some situations you have the right to refuse to work. To learn more about California OSHA laws call CAL/OSHA Consultation Services in Sacramento, CA at:**1-800-963-9424 or 916-263-0704**

# "YOUR RIGHTS"

What Employers Do Not
Want You To Know

### Sample Personal Evaluation

| | | | |
|---|---|---|---|
| **Employee Name:** | Jane A. Doe | **Date:** | January 8, 2_____ |
| **Employee Position:** | Office Manager | **Date:** | Last review: 01/08/2_____ |
| **Supervisor's Name:** | Betsy XYZ | **Title:** | Human Resources Manager - West |

**Employee Signature:** _____

**Directions:** *Please complete this evaluation and forward it to your manager one week before your review.*

## Achievement of Objectives

Rate the employee on a scale of 1 – 5 for each of the following skill areas:

1 – Insufficient, clear development needs
2 – Needs improvement
3 – Good, successful performance
4 – Excellent performance
5 – Exceptional performance

<table>
<tr><th colspan="2"></th><th>Rating</th><th>Comments (Sample Answers)</th></tr>
<tr><td rowspan="6">Core Skills</td><td>Communication</td><td>4</td><td>I communicate well with everybody in the office including vendors.</td></tr>
<tr><td>Team Skills</td><td>5</td><td>I am a team player. I am always assisting others when I can.</td></tr>
<tr><td>Leadership</td><td>4</td><td>I am fluid in this role. I have successfully been able to problem solve as well as integrate innovative ideas into my position.</td></tr>
<tr><td>Financial Management</td><td>4</td><td>I am open to learning more; and, my great budgeting skills have kept us in the black.</td></tr>
<tr><td>Organizational Building</td><td>5</td><td>I am great when it comes to creating organization from scratch. I have done so here and I am always open to learning new things.</td></tr>
<tr><td>Overall Core Skills</td><td>4</td><td>Objectively, I am still in the learning process and am willing to grow professionally. My core skills are: communication and organization.</td></tr>
</table>

**Responsibilities:** *List your (sample) major responsibilities of your current position.*

**Goals and Objectives:**

*Please list your goals and objectives for the next review period. (I.e. additional responsibilities, skills to acquire, training to complete, improvement areas to focus on etc.)*

**General Comments:**

*Get to know yourself well enough to present your core skills and abilites. Add sheets to explain your position more fully!*

# "YOUR RIGHTS"

♠♠♠

### What Employers Do Not
### Want You To Know

You are not a bad person. You show up for work on time and you do your job. Say you are in your tenth month, and your supervisor has yet to tell you anything negative or positive about how you are doing on your job. You should be worried! You used your hand-sheet from this guide to evaluate your employment and project input.

### Oh no! Why me?

You even worked overtime. So, why then are you about to be let go by your employer? Study these important clues and prepare yourself to get answers from your manager or supervisor when RED FLAGS go up!

1.  The boss has time for Nelly but no time for you. (Red Flag)

2.  You have no work, paper planes are piling up. (Red Flag)

3.  Nelly is doing your job; right in front of you. (Red Flag)

4.  Negative feedback, from everyone begins. (Red Flag)

5.  Red jelly doughnut drippings land on a classified ad of your job. (Red Flag)

**Tipsy time:** No. Do not get a drink, but think. Talk it out and get feed back from people at work you trust. Then ask to meet with your supervisor privately. Show her/him your hand-sheet input pointing out project participation and completion of projects that they may not have been aware of. And then, if nothing changes, start wisely looking for another job ***on your own personal time***. Use this guide to explore and evaluate your many job options. Check out the best and worst job list. Next time choose a career that is more suitable for your talent. Do not quit your job, ever.

## The Cooked Walk

Being fired canned, or let go is no laughing matter. However, the true reality of today's faced paced technological world is that more than a quarter of American workers will be fired at least once in their working career and that does not necessarily mean that it was "all" your fault. It is likely that as you are reading this book someone is being fired. I have done the cooked walk before and I have seen others do it before me.

# "YOUR RIGHTS"
### ♠♠♠
What Employers Do Not
Want You To Know

I maintain like many innocent workers that I never deserved it and the whole getting fired process is nothing short of mortifying and humiliating. Read how Nadine House handled her cook walk. See if you can avoid being the next to do the "Cooked Walk."

### Nadine House - How the Cooked Walk begins

I am Nadine House, a 43-year-old mother of 3 and wife of a disabled and unemployed veteran, and today I will be fired. Five O'clock arrived, on a Friday of course. The manager halted, and asked me, *"Can I see you in the Mount Everest Conference Room at five?"* I said, "yes". Mount Everest is the biggest conference room of four in the company. Each room was named after a famous mountain, and the idea for that was mine. I remember the day we mulled over names. I was the captain of the team then. Everyone loved it when my great idea for conference rooms day rendered me to be the company's innovative winner. I won a gold plaque with my name on it that my whole family was proud of. That jubilation lasted about a week. How soon they forget. Now, a few years later, they picked the *Mount Everest Conference* room to fire me in. I had read that companies usually like to fire employees in the boardroom, or someplace that would allow the employee to call somebody a rotten bitch or dirty bastard and I never thought it would ever happen to me. The article I read said that they usually let you say two or three cuss words. Then of course, you have to stop venting and swearing or they, (meaning the employer) will call security.

When the firing committee left, I looked around my cubicle for the last time and I wanted to cry but I did not want my team members at work to see me leaving in tears. I paced myself slowly. *No need to hurry when the consequences of my career had already been decided.* At 4:59 p.m., I marched slowly past two tired gray Cannon fax machines and one dirty white water cooler with the light blue spigot for cold water, and the bright red spigot for the hot water side that never worked. I was on my way to face the firing squad. I felt like the dead woman walking when I took the cooked walk. Depression caused my heads up will to shatter. I felt numb as my chin bowed into my chest. News spreads fast. Glaring eyes sat on top the brims of row after row of awful gray cubicles. The curious co-workers were the lucky ones. They were now the gainfully employed and they watched me, the dead woman walking move downward to my destiny. Depression, embarrassment and humiliation afforded me a hazy cloud to block out the onlookers. People began to whisper, "*what happened?*" They knew it was over for me. After five years with the company, sales were low.

# "YOUR RIGHTS"

♠♠♠

### What Employers Do Not
### Want You To Know

The title, *"Retail Manager"* had been on the cutting block for a year. I was surprised this day had not come sooner. Slow sales? What could I do? I wanted to cry, and go to the bathroom, but the walk, that awful walk down that long hallway decorated with picture after picture of successful sales ingenues, took forever. My nerves were shattered. Mount Everest housed the HR manager who was sitting with my supervisor Darlene, both were drinking the last of Hills Brothers burnt coffee offerings.

The HR person smoothed her pale white hands over a fat Manila paper trail file. "Go ahead and sit in the gray chair Nadine," Darlene said. I sat. Next, my supervisor got up and closed the conference room door. When she returned to her seat, she offered me some burnt coffee. I said no, intentionally leaving off the "thank you". I eased into the hard gray chair and held back my tears as the sudden strong urge to release myself lifted my butt out of the chair. I bit my lip. Then I straightened my back to hear their excuses on why I was about to be fired.

I became humble as I listened to the manager tell the HR person that I was dumb and could not catch on to the new sales approach in the company.

Her statements belied the three years I had been honored as the employee of the year. She said that my inability to catch on quickly and be a team player was the reason that they were letting me go. I had wanted to learn the new procedures faster. I worked overtime to learn pages and pages of retail new-age objectives. Unfortunately, I had not received the proper training for the new sales objectives. Therefore, I failed by their estimation and before long there was talk in the industry, that they were replacing me with a twenty-year old. Nevertheless, I accepted my fate and held back my tears. I was offered and I rejected the severance package because I was going to fight for my rights. I had my own paper trail and eyewitnesses to prove my case, and I had three employee of the year awards. The company I loved discarded me, and I knew it was going to be hard for me to find another job over forty.

After the firing, I hired a big firm employment law attorney to file claims for overtime and age discrimination, intentional infliction of emotional distress and defamation of character. My great work record forced the employer to defend letting me go. Their policy was inconsistent. Their contract with me was clearly implied and their mission statement all but promised me a permanent job if I stayed in my job over two years. Two years later at the trial the employer came prepared with documentation. However, I knew my rights and what they had was insufficient according to the jury. I had documented better than they had.

My performance evaluations were excellent. Furthermore, I had the chance to show the jury my awards. I was able to present cogent evaluation "comments" input, times, dates and witnesses to corroborate my side of the firing. Seven out of twelve jurors cried openly in court for me. The judge hated the employer's excuse for letting me go. However, most important of all, I had employment laws on my side. I was not nasty to my former employer. I was however, prepared. Armed with facts and the truth, in the end I won three times my former salary. In this case, the lawyer settled to keep the employer from filing a drawn out appeal. I was happy that I had kept all my smart notes on my snappy *"My rights," hand-sheet*. From the moment my employer stopped listening to my input at work, I wrote everything down. My employer called me dumb, and I wrote that down and helped my case significantly by writing down all dates and times. In essence, I was merely a human being trying to make an honest living for my family and I hung in there and won!

**NEWSFLASH!** *Judges do not like it when employers fire employees for not catching on or for not knowing how to do the job! Nadine intuitively took advantage of her rights. For three-years she kept important e-mails and she wrote things down. Keeping her files at home, Nadine was a good employee who ended up being a victim of circumstances. The judges, administrative law judges, and employee advocates of the world want to hear that you are at work everyday as Nadine was. They want to know that you tried to do your job right and that you were dependable as Nadine was. They want to see that you did not voluntarily quit your job or threaten your supervisor, and if you tangibly prove to the judge all of that and show them all your accumulated great note keeping facts, chances are you will win your case just as Nadine won her case. Your employer will lose against you with a reprimand from the court. Win or lose, you can then take pride that you did the right thing for you.*

**_Remember:_** If you need an employment lawyer, NELA is the country's only professional organization that is exclusively comprised of lawyers who represent individual employees in cases involving employment discrimination and other employment-related matters. The headquarters is located in San Francisco, California.

Consult the yellow pages of your telephone book, or go look for one on the computer[3]. I am not a lawyer, but I can help you with the basic fundamental tools to help yourself that I have acquired in my long work history. For

---

[3] Again an excellent source for finding an employment law attorney is the National Employment Lawyers Association (NELA) at www.nela.org

more fun secrets read on, and make sure to run wallet size copies of sample letters and charts and other fun things from this guide to carry with you at all times.

## More tips:

You have the right to sue an employer for ***"wrongful disciplinary actions,"*** even if you do not get fired!

**Example:**     One day Susan X was humiliated by her boss when he called her a fat pig and then he directed outrageous, offensive slurs at her. After this humiliating circumstance, Susan asked the Department of Human Resources to move her to another work area. When Susan X was granted her move she attempted to go back to her old cubicle to pack her things. Next, her old boss refused to let her get her personal property, and then he told her he knew she was not coming back, so he threw all of her family pictures away.

*Susan X did all the right things. She reported her boss immediately to the right personnel. Then, she stayed calm and professional. After a complete investigation of the aforementioned matter, Susan kept her job and won $75,000.00 in damages for her old bosses "wrongful disciplinary" actions, humiliation, defamation of character, and for possibly a few other things as well. Remember to always be cool.*

1.   Tell the offender to cease and desist

2.   Record such events in your diary

3.   Report it immediately to the Department of Human Resources

4.   Get names, dates and correct times of all witnesses to such an event

# "YOUR RIGHTS"
♠♠♠
What Employers Do Not
Want You To Know

## KNOW WHAT CLAIM TO FILE

☐ A regular California claim if you worked in California in a job covered by the unemployment insurance law even if you now reside outside California.

☐ A federal claim if your employment was in civilian work for the federal government or as a member of the Armed Forces (*benefit costs are paid from federal funds*).

☐ An interstate claim if earnings were in another state. If you worked in another state in the last 24 months, you may be able to file a claim. This includes the District of Columbia, Canada, Puerto Rico, and the Virgin Islands.

☐ A combined wage claim if you have earnings in more than one state in specified times. This type of claim could increase your Unemployment Insurance benefits. For base periods and more, call one of the numbers below.

**Unemployment Insurance Call Information:**

| | | |
|---|---|---|
| English: 1-800-300-5616 | Vietnamese: | 1-800-547-2058 |
| Spanish: 1-800-326-8937 | TTY (Non Voice) | 1-800-815-9387 |
| Cantonese 1-800-547-3506 | | |

WHY? Your employer pays into this insurance to provide you with an income when you are out of work through no fault of your own.

Internet Services:

www.edd.ca.gov

## Recording more of your time

All the time that you put into resolving a workplace problem are considered "hours worked." Therefore, the employer is required to pay you regular rates and regular overtime for over 8 hours. Code Sections 200,1174 1195.5; Industrial Welfare Commission Orders 1-3, 6-10, 13, 14 Title 29 U.S. Code Sections 201-219 785.42.

# "YOUR RIGHTS"
♠♠♠
What Employers Do Not
Want You To Know

**Question:**     The most important person you should know at work:

*Jeopardy Answer*: **Who is the Human Resources Manager**

The Human Resources Manager does a lot more than file department records and conduct new employee orientations. This is the most important resource you should know in the company. Therefore, it will not hurt you to learn who this person is and make them your strongest work alliance.

The Human Resources person develops and administers HR plans and procedures for all personnel. This person organizes and controls essentially all activities of the department and participates in developing departmental goals, objectives and systems with assistance to the corporate executives in the company. Employment laws guide this person strictly. In common words: The Human Resources Manager has a powerful influence in the company and she or she maintain imminent power in settling employment and money issues with you more swiftly really than anyone else in the company. Presidents, and Company vice presidents, do not want to deal with run of the mill problems that can be resolved below their level. A good HR person has excellent bargaining knowledge, and superb resolution skills.

The Human Resources Manager, updates compensation programs, and rewrites job descriptions as necessary; conducts annual salary surveys and develops merit pool (salary budgets). This person is the most prominent guide you have to get your point across to middle and upper management. *Find out who the HR person is and if you want to take them to Starbucks one day, that would be a great strategic move on your part.* Seriously, she/he controls personnel policies, procedures and they regularly update the employee handbook manuals and it will never hurt for the HR person to know first hand what a great employee you are. If you have a question regarding any of your employment rights, it is the HR person's job to have or get the answers for you. Generally, the Human Resources Department maintains all affirmative action program; files the annual EEO-1; in conformance with state and federal regulations.

# "YOUR RIGHTS"
♠♠♠
## What Employers Do Not
## Want You To Know

**Smart share tip:**

*When the judge saw how behind in times Rick's former job was with payroll record keeping, she tore into the company over everything from having illegal pay stubs to why the hell they had him working for straight time on Thanksgiving Day. The judge said: "You paid Rick Davis under time here. Then, you paid him over time there. Which time is the right time for Rick Davis?" The HR person had never been a real professional and in the judge's estimation, she did not like Rick Davis. Just like the company in question, she never took Rick's employment wage rights seriously. Wearing a white, fishing cap, and an orange windbreaker, with a pair of faded, blue Levi's her attire in itself was an insult to the judge. To make matters worse, this HR person was visibly shaken. After she lifted off her cap, her attempts to tame her wild blond curls was a lost cause. She told the judge that payroll was not her job. Rick wanted to laugh, but Rick read this guide and he showed up in front of the judge prepared. Rick had seen a few episodes of Judge Judy and Judge Mathis and he knew how to behave in a court of law. Rick spoke only when he was asked to by the judge and he addressed all of his answers to the magistrate with "yes sir/ma'am" or "no sir/ma'am" and he made no comments to his employer. The grilling of the human resources person by the judge began to feel better than a cold bath on a hot day to Rick Davis! He had been denied his overtime for over two years and as much as he enjoyed it, memories of his long fight to fairness quieted his need for expression. Preparedness, professionalism and great note taking rendered a sound judgement in favor of Rick Davis in the full amount of $36,000.00.*

# "YOUR RIGHTS"
♠♠♠
What Employers Do Not
Want You To Know

◻

CHAPTER 4
**_Required Work Posters_**
& More
Required Posters

The following is a chart of current required posters for California employers. You have the most current posters

if you have a _California Chamber of Commerce Employer Poster with "2005" in the upper right corner._

Remember: <u>Note: Apply all new material to your current year's law</u>

The chart is arranged in the order the posters appear on the Chamber's Employer Poster, available at

http://www.calchamberstore.com.

Required posters must be displayed at each work site and must be in an area accessible to all employees.

Generally speaking, the most current version of each poster must be displayed. State and federal agencies

periodically make changes to required posters. To find out about poster updates after the date of this printing go

to http://www.hrcalifornia.com/poster.

Log 300 - Not every employer must comply with Cal/OSHA's Log 300 record keeping requirements.

◉ Find out whether your company is required to record workplace injuries and illnesses using the Exempt

Wizard at http://www.hrcalifornia.com/log300

◉ Download the Log 300 forms from _http://www.hrcalifornia.com/log300_

Other - Unique posters and notices may be required depending on certain circumstances such as heavy

equipment or forklifts, chemical use, and government contracts.

*Both the state and federal minimum wage posters must be posted, even though California's minimum wage is

currently higher than the federal minimum wage.

<u>Your smart samples of "exempt" and "non-exempt" employees</u>

| TYPICAL EXEMPT JOBS | TYPICAL NON-EXEMPT JOBS |
|---|---|
| • Department Head | • Data Entry Clerk |
| • Financial Consultant | • Front Desk Receptionist |
| • Doctor or Physician | • Customer Service Clerk |
| • Credit Manager | • Secretary |
| • Account Executive | • Bank Teller |
| • Personal Director | • Newspaper Reporter |
| • Lawyer (Attorney) | • Bookkeeper |
| • Tax Specialist | • Trainee |

# "YOUR RIGHTS"

♠♠♠

### What Employers Do Not
### Want You To Know

| Poster Title | Who Must Post? | Source | Version/Date |
|---|---|---|---|
| Emergency Phone Numbers | All employers | Department of Industrial Relations www.dir.ca.gov | S-500 March 1990 |
| Pay Day Notice | All employers | Department of Industrial Relations www.dir.ca.gov | No version number No date |
| Safety and Health Protection on the job | All employers | Department of Industrial Relations, Division of Occupational Safety & Health www.dir.ca.gov/dosh | No version number August 2003 |
| Notice to Employees- Injuries Caused by Work | All employers | Department of Workers' Compensation www.dir.ca.gov/dwc | DWC Form 7 (8/1/04) |
| Discrimination or Harassment in Employment Is Prohibited by Law | All employers | Department of Fair Employment & Housing www.dfeh.ca.gov | DFEH 162 (04/04) |
| California Minimum Wage* | All employers | Industrial Welfare Commission www.dir.ca.gov/IWC | MW-2001 |
| Federal Minimum Wage* | All employers | Federal Department of Labor www.dol.gov | WH Pub 1088 Revised October 1996 |
| Pregnancy Disability Leave (5-49 employees) | Employers of five to 49 employees | Department of Fair Employment & Housing www.dfeh.ca.gov | DFEH 100-20 (01/00) |
| Family Care and Medical Leave (CFRA Leave) and Pregnancy Disability Leave | Employers of 50 or more employees and all "public agencies" | Department of Fair Employment & Housing www.dfeh.ca.gov | DFEH 100-21 (01/00) |
| Your Rights Under the Federal Family and Medical Leave Act of 1993 | Employers of 50 or more employees and all "public agencies" | Federal Department of Labor www.dol.gov | WH Pub 1420 Revised August 2001 |
| Equal Employment Opportunity is the Law | All employers | Equal Employment Opportunity Commission www.doi.gov | EEOC-P/E-1 (Revised 9/02) |
| Time Off for Voting | All employers. Must be posted for 10 days preceding statewide election. | California Secretary of State www.ss.ca.gov | No version number No date |
| Notice Employee Polygraph Protection Act | All employers | Federal Department of Labor www.dol.gov | WH Pub 1462 September 1988 2001 |
| Notice to Employees- Unemployment Insurance, State Disability Insurance, And Paid Family Leave | Most employers | Employment Development Department www.edd.ca.gov | DE 1857A Rev. 35 (10/03) |
| Whistleblower Poster | All employers | Office of the California Attorney General | No version number (01/04) |
| Log and Summary of Occupational Injuries and Illness (Log 300) | High hazard Employers of 10 or more employees, summary to be posted February 1 - April 30. | Department of Industrial Relations, Division of Occupational Safety & Health www.dir.gov/dosh | Revised 4/2004 |
| Your Wage Orders (17) | All employers must post the industry specific Wage Order for their business | Department of Industrial Relations www.dir.ca.gov www.hrcalifornia.com/wage orders | There are 17 Wage Orders, with various version dates. Check HR California.com/wageorders for current. |

# "YOUR RIGHTS"
♠♠♠
What Employers Do Not
Want You To Know

**Readers note**:

IWC Wage Orders - All employers must post the industry-specific Wage Order appropriate to their business, with a "Summary" in front of it. Visit http://www.hrcalifornia.com/wageorderwizard for help with selecting the correct wage order for your business.

**Smart tips**:

1. Employees working 20 hours or more a week are usually eligible for holiday pay.

2. Holiday pay is your regular straight time rate for the number of hours in an 8-hour workday.

3. An employee typically has to work the day before the holiday and the day after the holiday to get paid for the holiday.

4. When the holiday crashes on a Saturday, the preceding Friday is then usually considered the Company holiday. When the holiday falls on Sunday, then the next Monday will usually be the Company holiday.

5. Out of paid status, employees are not eligible for holiday pay. So, wait until you are off your disability or layoff to get holiday pay benefits.

6. Regular employees who work on a holiday will get one and one half times their regular pay rate. Biweekly employees who work a holiday that falls on their regular day off will be paid at twice their regular rate and receive another day off with pay. (*Talk to your HR person for more details about holiday pay. Different companies may have varying policies regarding holidays and pay.*)

**Standard holiday policy**

Some players go right into a job and the first thing they want to know is: "When is the next holiday. Be smart and recognize that everybody ain't celebrating Martin Luther King Holiday, (especially) in private industry. So, if it is your partner's birthday, or your mama's birthday, chances are it is not a holiday for the Company!

7. Make sure that payroll knows holiday pay is not to be considered hours worked in the figuring of overtime.

**Reminder:**

Employee coverage via union or negotiated contracts will follow holiday pay as is laid out in specific bargaining terms. If you are an active member of a union, meet with your Shop Steward, or delegate to acquire a full picture of your union contract rights.

# "YOUR RIGHTS"
♠♠♠
What Employers Do Not
Want You To Know

**Claim it, it is yours**

Unfortunately, many workers have had to build up the gall to fight and to that end, many survivors have won big time exercising their special employment rights. You need to know that winning is possible and you need to know that you can get what is rightfully yours. As much as we would like to enjoy the honor system and trust our employer, times have changed and the need for continual evidence forces us to write things down. Know your rights, claim it, it's yours and you have the power to get it. An employee without rights is like a phantom without his mask. Be ready for the employer and the employer will be ready to treat you with the fairness and respect that you deserve on the job.

**Your good record keeping**

At the beginning and in the middle of this guide, you will see the personal time keeping record I have created for you where you can record all of your work time regular and overtime. Copy this form and use it daily to record your time and work events and the hours you spent resolving work related issues. **Reminder**: remember to write special notes for yourself and keep records because tangible facts is a great way to get promoted on the job, or government agencies give special credence to your great calendar and note taking. Having great records is almost a certain way to get you the win you are seeking to prove overtime hours that you may not have gotten paid for.

**Your guiding eyes**

I want to be your guiding eyes. I want to assist you in keeping track of your job, to monitor your wages and make sure that not a dime of your overtime payment sits in your employer's bank account earning interest (*for them*) or the rich one(s) on the golf courses across America. Recently, a dear friend of mine had a hearing with the Department of Labor. My friend was prepared to fight for her overtime wages, and here is what she found out!

**Reminder:**        It is required under federal law that the employer pay a "non-exempt worker at least one and one half times their regular rates of pay for all hours worked in excess of 40 hours per week. In California, non-exempt employees who work in excess of 8 hours per day earn time and one half for all time worked after 8 hours in one given day and this time is doubled for holiday work.

CHAPTER 5
**Employee Sherlock Must**

**Preparation is key:**

If you ever go to battle with the employer, there are some very important facts that you will need to know:

**Laws that protect you at work:**

| | | |
|---|---|---|
| The Pregnancy Discrimination Act | Title V11 of the Civil Rights Act of 1964 | Equal Pay Act 1963 |
| Age Discrimination in Employment Act 1967 | Americans with Disability Act (ADA) | |

1. Know what the employee handbook says - (*never throw this book away*). Understand the general company policy, statement of goals, working hours. Understand the policy for non-disclosure, procedural policy, pay periods and performance evaluations. Find out what the safety rules are and follow them to the tee. Have respect for company property and telephones. Never make personal calls without permission from your supervisor. At work turn your cell phone off!

2. Know who the management decision makers in the company are - (get a copy of the companies organization chart from their Intranet site and take it home and store it before things go bad.) You need to know where your bargaining power lies, and who the ***powerful, decision making professionals are***, including the HR person, vice president, president, CEO, CIO and all company lenders/shareholders. If you are in a union, ask the shop steward to explain foreign policy to you in terms that you will understand. If you know who puts up front money to keep the company going, it can be an immense bargaining tool for you later.

3. Find out through public records if there are claims against your employer with the Better Business Bureau to use for your advantage, before you submit a demand letter for payment of a claim.

# "YOUR RIGHTS"
♠♠♠
What Employers Do Not
Want You To Know

4.      Be aware that (anyone) can write a demand letter to an employer. You don't need an attorney to put someone on notice. Use your Internet savvy to find sample letters on the Internet to help you do things the right way. Key: be prepared.

5.      Know who is the Department of Human Resources Manager.

6.      Know whom the lawyers for the company are and research them.

7.      Know the company policy towards your protected classes. If you are over (40), find out about age discrimination policy and procedures.

8.      Research issues thoroughly before presenting your case to the employer. *Tip:* the library in your community is a great resource for employment issues and law.

**Note: Apply all new material to current year's law**

### SEXUAL HARASSMENT TRUTH/FACTS

Sexual Harassment is against the law. The day you begin your new job read the employee manual and then learn what the Company policy is on harassment and sexual harassment. REMEMBER: It is your right to say no to a person that pursues you on the job. Many companies have stringent policies against sexual harassment. Consult your employee handbook to find out what the policy is and hold the Company accountable to their written policy regarding sexual harassment. Remember to report harassment, and sexual harassment immediately to your supervisor. Tell the harasser to cease and desist. (See the sample cease and desist letter to the offender below.) All employees are entitled to work in an environment that is free of harassment.

IMPORTANT NEW LAW

**AB1825 Sexual Harassment Training**

*As of 2005, Employers with 50 or more employees must provide 2 hours of training and education to all supervisory employees within one year of January 1, 2005. An employer is exempt if it has provided sexual harassment training and education to employees after January 1, 2003. Effective January 1, 2006, each employer must provide sexual harassment training and education to each supervisory employee once every 2 years.* **Note: Apply all new material after aforementioned dated to current year's law**

**Smart reporting do's:**

1.   Tell harasser that: "*your actions are not welcome I find them offensive, please stop.*"

2.  Document harassment, obtain offensive writings, pictures or emails pertaining to the harasser's offenses to give copies of to his supervisor.

3.  Report harasser's offensive behavior immediately to a supervisor.

**NOTE:**   Most companies have a policy to act on discrimination and harassment charges immediately. It is the supervisor's responsibility to report the complaint to the Department of Human Resources. Usually, a prompt investigation will ensue.

### Smart reporting don'ts:

1.  Never take matters into your own hands

2.  Never threaten the harasser

3.  Never get violent on the job or anywhere

4.  Never add things to your charges about a person that are not true

### Smart info in proving sexual harassment on the job

- **Sexual Harassment:**

*RE: Unreasonable Conduct*

Point #1        "If harassed by unreasonable conduct, the most important evidence you can present is that you let the harasser know that you found his conduct unreasonable; and, that he persisted to violate the standard you set.

THE VICTIMS FACTUAL ACTIONS:

- **Proving Sexual Harassment:**

*Evidence I told harasser behavior unreasonable*

Point #2        "Evidence you told harasser he was behaving unreasonably; dated entry in your journal; a copy of the letter I sent."

THE VICTIMS FACTUAL ACTIONS:

- **Law in Proving Sexual Harassment:**

*Evidence Victim reported harasser to Co-workers*

THE VICTIMS FACTUAL ACTIONS:

# "YOUR RIGHTS"
♠♠♠
What Employers Do Not
Want You To Know

- **Law in Proving Sexual Harassment:**

*Evidence Harasser's conduct created offensive/intimidating work environment*

- **More of Proving Sexual Harassment:**

*Evidence harasser's touching was severe, etc.,*

THE VICTIMS FACTUAL "SUFFERING" VIA HARASSER'S ACTIONS:

- **Proving Sexual Harassment with Evidentiary Materials:**

*Evidence of direct injury as a result of harasser's actions, and persistence to cause harm.*

### How Sally Exercised Her Rights.

During the two-year course of her employment at her former Company Sally, was fondled by the CEO six times. The first time he touched her inappropriately, Sally, asked him to stop and then she reported his conduct to her supervisor. After an in-house investigation disproved Sally's charges, the next time it happened, the CEO told Sally to *"deal with it"* because no one had believed her the first time. He further stated to her that if she wanted to keep her job and get a promotion next year to *"ship up or shape out"*. Then he made sure when he stroked Sally the next five times that nobody was around to see it. Hence, Sally was left with no witnesses to the CEO's detestable behavior. In due course, Sally became ill. Consequently, she started receiving professional counseling for the residual effects of the CEO's persistent harassing behavior. Sally had a stellar work record, and had never been written up or reprimanded by her supervisor before. In fact, her job performance appraisals had all been rated excellent. After the ill-fated investigation, Sally's work output was down. Her work efforts had clearly suffered counter-actively because of the CEO's ongoing actions.

One year after Sally told her supervisor and the Department of Human Resources about the CEO she was fired without cause. Determined to exercise her civil rights under Title VII, Sally contacted each chain of command in her employ to reconcile her claims to no avail. Then Sally wrote a certified letter to Department of Human Resources exemplifying her administrative remedies in accordance with the Company's employment handbook policy.

When all of her administrative opportunities were (fully) expended, within 30 days,

# "YOUR RIGHTS"
♠♠♠
## What Employers Do Not
## Want You To Know

The Department of Fair Employment & Housing, (DFEH) made an appointment to review the facts of Sally's case. On the day of her appointment, Sally presented to them a well-documented case and the Department took her complaint. Later, a copy of the charge was given to Sally. Then, another copy was mailed to her Company.

A week after the charge was filed, Sally found an employment law attorney. Sally, then asked the Department of Fair Employment & Housing, *(in writing)* to dismiss her charge and issue to her a right-to-sue letter against her former Company. Sally now had one year from the date of the issuance of the *right-to-sue* letter to sue her old Company. When the skilled employment law attorney saw how well-prepared Sally was he took her case immediately on contingency leaving Sally free of having to deal with her former Company again.

With attention to detail, *great note taking*, itemizations of correct times and dates, and excellent performance evaluations the attorney acknowledged that Sally had made his job easy by handling her case so well. Great preparation, determination and an excellent work record forced Sally's former employer to settle out of court with her for a total sum of $75,000.00.

**NOTE: Before you hire an attorney, check them out through the California Bar Association.**

## Retaliation:

Your job can not legally harass you for filing an innocent complaint because it is against the law. Your complaint is in good faith. You participated <u>fully</u> in the Department of Human Resource's investigation, and you told your harasser to cease and desist and you can prove it because you wrote it down in your diary with your other corroborating evidence. If your employer fires you for exercising your rights under a protected class their retaliation against you will be considered a "separate" violation under the Civil Rights Act under title VII of the employment law.

## MORE IMPORTANT NEW LAW:

August 11, 2004 Amendment to SB 1809

"Sue Your Boss" Law

The original law, effective 1/1/04, under Senate Bill 796, allowed an employee and their attorney to sue for alleged violations and bypass state agency enforcement. SB 796 created penalties for every Labor Code violation and enabled the employee to share in any penalty awarded by the court.

The court could also award attorneys' fees. Not surprisingly, this law resulted in a flurry of anti-employer lawsuits, as hungry attorneys saw an opportunity to cash in on the bill.

## Anti-retaliation provisions

In order to protect employees from discrimination or retaliation for giving a notice alleging a violation to the Agency or the employer, or filing a lawsuit, **SB1809** amended Labor Code section 98.6. Protections are included in matters involving:

### Employment

1. Discharge or threat of discharge

2. Demotion

3. Suspension

4. Terms and conditions of employment

5. Training opportunities

**NOTE:** *The protection is extended to employees who testify or are about to testify about a notice or claim. It applies whether the claim is filed on the individual's own behalf or on behalf of others.*

# "YOUR RIGIITS"

♠♠♠

What Employers Do Not
Want You To Know

### SAMPLE CEASE AND DESIST LETTER TO OFFENDER

January 5, 200_____

John Doe, CEO
XXXX
Company XXX
Concord, CA 94520

Mr John Doe:

On January 02, 200_____ I told you that I was not interested in you. After work on the aforementioned date you pulled up to the bus stop at 5:30 p.m. demanding that I get into the car with you. When I refused, you got out of your car and then you approached me. When I said, I was going to call the police you left. John, this is harassment. I find your actions extremely troublesome and offensive. Therefore, for the second time I am asking you to stop, cease, and desist. If you contact me or stalk me again, I will report you to the police and to your supervisor.

Jane Doe
Witnessed by: Carla_____     Date: _____

Notarized by: _____

# "YOUR RIGHTS"
♠♠♠
What Employers Do Not
Want You To Know

□

## CHAPTER 6
## DEPARTMENT OF FAIR EMPLOYMENT & HOUSING
## YOUR KEYS TO THE MAILBOX AND MORE

**(1-800-884-1684)**
*WWW.DFEH.CA.GOV*
State of California

When you have been discriminated against or sexually harassed on your job, you are exhausted! Therefore, you will not have the energy to read all the materials to do things right so that you can win your case. You are reading this guide to implement procedures in the right order to present a cogent case. Don't worry! I am going to break down to you how you must approach the Department of Fair Employment and Housing in a professional manner and in a way that you don't have to stress on. *We will call the following section, Your checklist √*

> *When the checklist of events as listed below have been reported and exhausted in accordance with the stated procedures of your office manual - you are then ready to file with the DFEH and or the Department of Labor. Many human resource department managers are fair and (do not want you to file cases that will lead to protracted litigation against their Company,) Remember: tell the truth, keep copious notes, dates, places, times and witnesses.*

| | |
|---|---|
| 1. √I was discriminated against or harassed | 6. √I reported incident to the Department of Human Resources as soon as the events occurred. |
| 2. √I reported it to my supervisor | 7. √I reported the incident to all chains of commands to no avail, and the investigation was closed. |
| 3. √I wrote down the events and requested an investigation. I cooperated fully in investigation. | 8. √I have exhausted all of my in office remedies in accordance with my companies policies as written in the employee handbook and still I have not been treated fairly, I am being retaliated against. |
| 4. √I advised the harasser to cease and desist/behavior; I have times, dates, witnesses. | 9. √I created a binder, on my own time to memorialize all actions in my case. I have given my employer a period to respond to settle my case. I have received no response. I have kept everything in order by dates/times. |
| 5. √My supervisor has not helped me fully. | 10. √My checklist is completed. I will inform the Department of Human Resources in writing that I am going to file a case with the Department of Fair Employment & Housing. If I am ignored, fired, or dismissed, I will proceed forward. |

# "YOUR RIGHTS"
♠♠♠
What Employers Do Not
Want You To Know

Your checklist is completed, and, now you are ready to proceed on. You are prepared to file your claim. You

have exhausted all of your administrative remedies, (*in accordance with the Company manual.*) Still your case

has not been rightfully resolved. Exhaust all in-house means before filing a complaint with the Department of

Fair Employment & Housing. With her attorney, she applied for a "Right-to-sue" notice. Review the application

below to see what questions you will be asked if you have a case.

# "YOUR RIGHTS"
♠♠♠
What Employers Do Not
Want You To Know

## SAMPLE LAST LETTER TO EMPLOYER
## BEFORE FILING WITH OUTSIDE AGENCIES

**CERTIFIED MAIL/EMAIL**

XYZ Company                                              January 17, 20_____
Attn: President, Yoo
P.O. Box XXX
Los Angeles, California 90210

Dear Mr. Yoo:

I have completed the following actions in accordance with your grievance policy as stated on pages 35 & 36 of your *Employee Handbook*:

❑   I reported discrimination to my supervisor the day it happened on 11/30/03.
❑   On 12/18/04 I appropriately submitted your form #CS92-05 to Kathy Doe in the Department of Human Resources.
❑   On 12/07/05, I met with you. Then on 01/11/2005, (the date you said you would get back to me), I heard nothing from you. On that date, Kathy said you ended my employment without cause.

To date, I have followed your complaint process according to policy down to the letter. Still, my grievance has been overlooked and has not been settled.

I sincerely want to resolve these issues in house. Please contact me at 310-565-XXXX in five days to discuss resolution of the wrongful termination, loss of overtime wages and other employment issues. Otherwise, on January 24, 2005, I will carry my petition to the *Department of Labor* and the *Department of Fair Employment & Housing* and *the Equal Employment Opportunity Commission*, where I am sure I will get fair resolution of my discrimination issues and wage losses.

Very truly yours,

John X. Doe

www.dfeh.ca.gov
**TTY #(800) 700-2320**

☐ 1001 Tower Way, Suite 250
Bakersfield, CA 93309-1586
**H** (661) 395-2729

☐ 1320 East Shaw Avenue, Suite #150
Fresno, CA 93710-7919
**C** (559) 244-4760

☐ 611 West Sixth Street, Suite 1500
Los Angeles, CA 90017-3116
**B** (213) 439-6799

☐ 1515 Clay Street, Suite #701
Oakland, CA 94612-2512
**M** (510) 622-2941

☐ 2000 "O" Street, Suite #120
Sacramento, CA 95814-5212
**E** (916) 445-5523

☐ 1845 S. Business Ctr Dr., Suite #127
San Bernardino, CA 92408-3426
**J** (909) 383-4373

☐ 350 W. Ash Street, Suite 950
San Diego, CA 92101-3440
**D** (610) 645-2681

☐ 121 Spear Street, Suite #430
San Francisco, CA 94105-1581
**A** (415) 904-2303

☐ 111 North Market Street, Suite #810
San Jose, CA 95113-1102
**G** (408) 277-1277

☐ 2101 E. 4th Street, Suite 255-B
Santa Ana, CA 92705-3814
**K** (714) 558-4266

☐ 1732 Palma Drive, Suite 200
Ventura, CA 93003-5796
**L** (805) 654-4514

*SMART SAMPLE DFEH INSTRUCTIONS. PLEASE READ CAREFULLY*

## "RIGHT-TO-SUE-NOTICE" INSTRUCTIONS

You have requested a "right-to-sue notice" from the Department of Fair Employment and Housing. The Fair Employment and Housing Act (FEHA), at Government Code section 12965, subdivision (b), requires that individuals must exhaust their administrative remedies with the Department of Fair Employment and Housing (DFEH) by filing a complaint and obtaining a "right-to-sue notice" from the Department before filing a lawsuit under the **FEHA**. DFEH will accept requests for an immediate **DFEH** "right-to-sue notice" from persons who have decided to proceed in court. Your DFEH complaint must be filed within one year from the last act of discrimination or you may lose your right to file a lawsuit under the **FEHA**.

The Process of proceeding directly to court without an investigation by DFEH is advisable only if you have an attorney. If you do not have an attorney, you can file a discrimination complaint with DFEH for investigation. If you decide to file a lawsuit later, you can still do so. If you wish to have your complaint investigated by DFEH, call 1-800-884-1684 for an appointment.

If you receive an immediate **DFEH** "right-to-sue notice," your complaint **will not be investigated by DFEH even if you later decide not to file a lawsuit.**

If you receive an immediate **DFEH** "right-to-sue notice," your complaint will not be dual-filed by DFEH with the U.S. Equal Employment Opportunity Commission (EEOC). DFEH complaints may be dual-filed with EEOC only if DFEH accepts the complaint for investigation. In order to receive a federal right-to-sue notice, you must file a complaint with EEOC WITHIN 30 days of your receipt of the DFEH "NOTICE OF CASE CLOSURE" OR WITHIN 300 DAYS OF THE ALLEGED DISCRIMINATORY ACT, WHICHEVER IS EARLIER. The telephone number for EEOC in Northern California is (415) 356-5100. The Southern California EEOC telephone number is (213) 894-1000.

EEOC enforces laws which prohibit discrimination based on race, religion, color, sex, national origin, age (40 or over) or disability. For race, religion, color, sex, national origin and disability complaints, **EEOC** has jurisdiction over employers who employ 15 or more persons. For age complaints, **EEOC** has jurisdiction over employers who employ 20 or more persons.

In signing the enclosed documents, you are acknowledging the following:

1) You have read and understood this letter.

2) You understand that once **DFEH** has issued an authorization to file a lawsuit DFEH will not investigate or reopen your complaint. **Furthermore, you have chosen not to exercise your option of having DFEH investigate your complaint and of electing court action later. You also understand you should have an attorney to file a lawsuit.**

3) You understand that **DFEH** will not file your complaint with EEOC, and that if you wish to obtain a federal right-to-sue notice from EEOC you must contact EEOC directly.

4) You have one year form the date of the **DFEH** "right-to-sue notice" to file a lawsuit.

If you wish to request an immediate DFEH "right-to-sue-notice" to file a lawsuit, complete the enclosed documents, and return them to the DFEH office checked in the margin of this letter. If you are filing against more than one Company or individual, you must submit a complaint form for each one. If there are not enough forms enclosed, please request additional copies from the office checked in the margin, or have additional copies made from the form enclosed. Please complete, sign and date, all of the complaint forms.

# "YOUR RIGHTS"
♠♠♠
What Employers Do Not
Want You To Know

## * * * EMPLOYMENT * * *

**COMPLAINT OF DISCRIMINATION UNDER**   DFEH _____
**THE PROVISIONS OF THE CALIFORNIA**                          DFEH USE ONLY
**FAIR EMPLOYMENT AND HOUSING ACT**

**CALIFORNIA DEPARTMENT OF FAIR EMPLOYMENT AND HOUSING**

| YOUR NAME (INDICATE MR. OR MS.) | TELEPHONE NUMBER (INCLUDE AREA CODE) |
|---|---|

ADDRESS

| CITY/STATE/ZIP | COUNTY | COUNTY CODE |
|---|---|---|

**NAMED IS THE EMPLOYER, PERSON, LABOR ORGANIZATION, EMPLOYMENT AGENCY, APPRENTICESHIP COMMITTEE, OR STATE OR LOCAL GOVERNMENT AGENCY WHO DISCRIMINATED AGAINST ME:**

| NAME | TELEPHONE NUMBER (INCLUDE AREA CODE) |
|---|---|

| ADDRESS | (DFEH USE ONLY) |
|---|---|

| CITY/STATE/ZIP | (COUNTY CODE) |
|---|---|

| NO. OF EMPLOYEES/MEMBERS (IF KNOWN) | DATE MOST RECENT OR CONTINUING DISCRMINATION TOOK PLACE (MONTH, DAY, AND YEAR)   (RESPONDENT CODE ) |
|---|---|

THE PARTICULARS ARE:

ON _____ I WAS

_____ FIRED
_____ LAID OFF
_____ DEMOTED
_____ HARASSED
_____ GENETIC CHARACTERISTICS TESTING
_____ FORCED TO QUIT

_____ DENIED EMPLOYMENT
_____ DENIED PROMOTION
_____ DENITED TRANSFER
_____ DENIED ACCOMMODATION
_____ IMPERMISSIBLE NON-JOB RELATED INQUIRY
_____ OTHER (SPECIFY) _____

_____ DENIED FAMILY OR MEDICAL LEAVE
_____ DENIED PREGNANCY LEAVE
_____ DENIED EQUAL PAY
_____ DENIED RIGHT TO WEAR PANTS
_____ DENIED PREGNANCY ACCOMODATION

BY

JOB TITLE (SUPERVISOR OR/MANAGER/PERSONNEL DIRECTOR/ETC.)

BECAUSE OF MY:

ON _____ I WAS

_____ SEX
_____ AGE
_____ RELIGION
_____ RACE/COLOR

_____ NATIONAL ORIGIN/ANCESTRY
_____ MARITAL STATUS
_____ SEXUAL ORIENTATION
_____ ASSOCIATION

_____ PHYSICAL DISABILITY
_____ MENTAL DISABILITY

_____ CANCER
_____ GENETIC CHARACTERISTIC

_____ (CIRCLE ONE ) FILING PROTESTING; PARTICIPATING IN NVESTIGATION (RETALIATION FOR)

_____ OTHER (SPECIFY)

BY

The reason given by

_____
**Name of Person and Job Title**

Was because of

_____

[please state
what you believe

_____

to be reason(s)]

_____

_____

I wish to pursue this matter in court. I hereby request that the Department of Fair Employment and Housing provide a right-to-sue notice. I understand that if I want a federal notice Of right-to-sue, I must visit the U.S. Equal Employment Opportunity Commission (EEOC) to file a complaint within 30 days of receipt of the DFEH "Notice of Case Closure," or within 300 days of the alleged discriminatory act, whichever is earlier.

# "YOUR RIGHTS"

## What Employers Do Not
## Want You To Know

I have not been coerced into making this request, nor do I make it based on fear of retaliation if I do not do so. I understand it is the Department of Fair Employment and Housing's Policy to not process or reopen a complaint once the complaint has been closed on the basis of "Complainant Elected Court Action."

I declare under penalty of perjury under the laws of the State of California that the foregoing is true and correct of my own knowledge except as to matters stated on my Information and belief, and as to those matters I believe it to be true.

Dated _____

_____

COMPLAINANT'S SIGNATURE

AT _____
    CITY

MY RIGHTS SMART GUIDE FOR EMPLOYEE IN THE KNOW
SAMPLE COMPLAINT FORM - DFEH-300-03 (01/03) DEPARTMENT OF FAIR EMPLOYMENT AND HOUSING

# "YOUR RIGHTS"

♠♠♠

What Employers Do Not
Want You To Know

## RIGHT-TO-SUE COMPLAINT INFORMATION SHEET

DFEH needs a separate signed complaint for each employer, person, labor organization, employment agency, apprenticeship committee, state or local
government agency you wish to file against. If you are filing against both a Company and an individual(s), please complete separate complaint forms naming
the Company or an individual in the appropriate area.

Please complete the following so that DFEH can process your complaint and for DFEH for statistical purposes, and return with your signed complaint(s):

**YOUR RACE:/ETHNICITY (Check one)**
—African-American
—African - Other
—Asian/Pacific Islander (specify)_____
—Caucasian (Non-Hispanic)
—Native American
—Hispanic (specify) _____

**YOUR PRIMARY LANGUAGE (specify)**

_____

**YOUR AGE:—**

**IF FILING BECAUSE OF YOUR NATIONAL ORIGIN/ANCESTRY,
YOUR NATIONAL (SPECIFY)**


_____

**IF FILING BECAUSE OF DISABILITY,
YOUR DISABILITY**
—AIDS
—Blood/Circulation
—Brain/Nerves/Muscles
—Digestive/Urinary/Reproduction
—Hearing
—Heart
—Limbs (Arms/Legs)
—Mental
—Sight
—Speech/Respiratory
—Spinal/Back

**IF FILING BECAUSE OF MARITAL STATUS
YOUR MARITAL STATUS: (check one)**
—Cohabitation
—Divorced
—Married
—Single
**IF FILING BECAUSE OF RELIGION,
YOUR RELIGION: (specify)**

_____

**IF FILING BECAUSE OF SEX, THE REASON:**
—Harassment
—Orientation
—Pregnancy
—Denied Right to Wear Pants
—Other Allegations (List)

**YOUR GENDER:**
—Female
—Male

**YOUR OCCUPATION:**
—Clerical
—Craft
—Equipment Operator
—Laborer
—Manager
—Paraprofessional
—Professional
—Sales
—Service
—Supervisor
—Technician

**HOW YOU HEARD ABOUT DFEH:**
—Attorney
—Bus/BART Advertisement
—Community Organization
—EEOC
—EDD
—Friend
—Human Relations Commission
—Labor Standards Enforcement
—Local Government Agency
—Poster
—Prior Contact with DFEH
—Radio
—Telephone Book
—TV
—DFEH Web Site

**DO YOU HAVE AN ATTORNEY?**
—Yes                —No

_____

**Your Signature**

_____

# "YOUR RIGHTS"
♠♠♠
What Employers Do Not
Want You To Know

The Fair Employment and Housing Act (FEHA), at Government Code section 12965, subdivision (b), requires

that individuals must exhaust their administrative remedies with the Department of Fair Employment and

Housing (DFEH) by filing a complaint and obtaining a "right-to-sue notice" from the Department before filing a

lawsuit under the FEHA. DFEH will accept requests for an immediate DFEH "right-to-sue notice" from persons

who have decided to proceed in court. Your complaint must be filed within one year from the last act of

discrimination or you may lose your right to file a lawsuit under the FEHA:

| DEPARTMENT OF FAIR EMPLOYMENT & HOUSING<br>1001 Tower Way, Suite #250<br>Bakersfield, CA 93309-1586<br>(661) 395-2729 | DEPARTMENT OF FAIR EMPLOYMENT & HOUSING<br>1320 E. Shaw Avenue, Suite #150<br>Fresno, CA 93710-7979<br>(559) 244-4760 |
|---|---|
| DEPARTMENT OF FAIR EMPLOYMENT & HOUSING<br>611 West Sixth Street, Suite #1500<br>Los Angeles, CA 90017-3116<br>(213) 439-6799 | DEPARTMENT OF FAIR EMPLOYMENT & HOUSING<br>1515 Clay Street, Suite #701<br>Oakland, CA 94612-2512<br>(510) 622-2941 |
| DEPARTMENT OF FAIR EMPLOYMENT & HOUSING<br>2000 "O" Street, Suite #120<br>Sacramento, CA 95814-5212<br>(916) 445-5523 | DEPARTMENT OF FAIR EMPLOYMENT & HOUSING<br>1845 S. Business Center Drive, Suite #127<br>San Bernardino, CA 92408-3426<br>(909) 383-4373 |
| DEPARTMENT OF FAIR EMPLOYMENT & HOUSING<br>350 W. Ash Street, Suite #950<br>San Diego, CA 92101-3440<br>(619) 645-2681 | DEPARTMENT OF FAIR EMPLOYMENT & HOUSING<br>121 Spear Street, Suite #430<br>San Francisco, CA 94105-1581<br>(415) 904-2303 |
| DEPARTMENT OF FAIR EMPLOYMENT & HOUSING<br>111 North Market Street, Suite #810<br>San Jose, CA 95113-1102<br>(408) 277-1277 | DEPARTMENT OF FAIR EMPLOYMENT & HOUSING<br>2101 East 4th Street, Suite #255-B<br>Santa Ana, CA 92705-3814<br>(714) 558-4266 |
| DEPARTMENT OF FAIR EMPLOYMENT & HOUSING<br>1732 Palma Drive, Suite #200<br>Ventura, CA 93003-5796<br>(805) 654-4514 | DEPARTMENT OF FAIR EMPLOYMENT & HOUSING<br>TTY (1-800) 700-2320 |

# "YOUR RIGHTS"
♠♠♠
What Employers Do Not
Want You To Know

## New and most recent 2005 Employment Law
## Articles to Read
### *FYI: Note: Apply all new material to current year's law*

Note: The following news was obtained from EL infonet.com an Employment Law information Network[4]

and does not completely, or absolutely provide specific details of what each of these findings fully

entail. For more detailed information about each of the following cases, visit the web-site and or consult

with an attorney for fuller legal clarification. Another great source to look up law can be found at

FindLaw.com. Following are samples of new interesting case law that could be important to you.

New:    <u>The employer not liable for constructive discharge for suggesting that an employee resign</u>

Source: E L infonet.com **Gibbons, Del Deo, Dolan, Griffinger & Vecchione, P.C. - May 11, 2005**

What does it mean?      -In Angeloni v. Diocese of Scranton, No. 03-4501, 2005 WL 616013 (3d Cir. March

17, 2005), the United States Court of Appeals for the Third Circuit affirmed the

district court's entry of summary judgment and ruled that employees *who resign from*

*their employment must demonstrate they were "constructively discharged" or they*

*will not prevail on their Title VII discrimination claims.*

New:    <u>The U.S. Supreme Court Rules Disparate Impact Claims Cognizable Under the ADEA</u>

Source: E L infonet.com **Gibbons, Del Deo, Dolan, Griffinger & Vecchione, P.C. - May 11, 2005**

What does it mean?      "Disparate impact" is a methodology for establishing that an employer has engaged in

discrimination against a specific group of employees or job applicants of the same

race. Ethnicity, religion or sex that does not require evidence that the employer

intended to discriminate.

New:    <u>FLSA Compliance</u>

Source: E L infonet.com **Michael Best & Friedrich LLP - May 10, 2005**

<u>Note: Apply all new material to current year's law</u>

# "YOUR RIGHTS"
♠♠♠
### What Employers Do Not
### Want You To Know

**What does it mean?** New Fair Labor Standards Act regarding overtime regulations in August of 2004, have many employers conducting internal audits of their wage and hour practices to determine if they are in compliance.

**New:** **In California Employers at Risk for Telephone Monitoring without Notice**

**Note: Apply all new material to current year's law - for employment laws are ever changing**

**Source: E L infonet.com  Vedder Price - April 29, 2005**

**What does it mean?** A California appeals court has held that an employee fired after his supervisor had secretly monitored a telephone conversation may sue his employer for invasion of privacy, wrongful termination and intentional infliction of emotional distress. (*In the 90's, 20,000 cases were filed for wrongful termination and the average award for the wronged was $500,000.00 up from 225,000 in 1986. Over 50% rewards in verdicts from the jury for the employee.*)

### Sitting On Top of Your Mail

**Mailing it right!**

When you are serious about your business, save yourself the time of screwing things up with a million and one mail options. Federal Express, Airborne, UPS and companies like them do a great job of picking up and delivering your mail. However, it does not get any better than the great *United States Post Office*. When you really want to do it right, consider the following trademark mailing options:

| Domestic Shipping Service Options | Regular Price | Speed |
|---|---|---|
| Overnight Guaranteed Packages (Express Mail®) | $13.65 and up | Next Day |
| 2-3 Day Packages (Priority Mail®), | $3.85 and up | 2-3 Days |
| Ground Packages (Parcel Post®, Media Mail® & more…) | $2.81 and up | 2-9 Days |

[4] http://www.elinfonet.com/recent.php

.

# "YOUR RIGHTS"

♠♠♠

What Employers Do Not
Want You To Know

◻

## CHAPTER 7
### STATE OF CALIFORNIA
### Department of Industrial Relations
### Division of Labor Standards Enforcement

### FILING A CLAIM

have kept all of your time cards and hand-sheets. You have been a good employee who still has not been

all of your due wages. You have approached and handled every facet of your business seriously, with

ity. Well, you need to know how the process of the Labor Department works. Before you read on remember

ip of this chapter: _**"Be calm, cool and collective always"**_. You are intelligent; you are exercising your rights

ou simply want to get what is yours. Payroll denied your claim. But, you know you are right. Therefore, at

interval in dealing with what is owed to you, you mailed certified letters and you can prove to the judge

your receipts, notes and written evidence that you do things in an orderly fashion. You kept your receipts.

ut the cost, time and dates of those receipts in your diary, and the judge is going to put weight on your

y stratagem. You know your rights and now you need to get the money your employer owes you and you

ious.

### ou are going to the Department of Labor

ou have wages or overtime that is due to you that has not been paid.

ou have reported this to your immediate supervisor/nothing was done.

u have reported this to your supervisor's boss and nothing was done.

u have appealed to each and every chain of command in your Company/nothing was done.

i have gone through the employee handbook a dozen times. You still have not been paid. No matter what

handbook says, all time worked MUST BE PAID. Never let the employer convince you that hours

ked are not compensible.

_you! You needed to know – now you are ready to take this job to the Labor Board - please read the_

_g and good luck!_

tchell, CDM3publisher.com

# "YOUR RIGHTS"

♠♠♠

What Employers Do Not
Want You To Know

(Continued)

| International Shipping - Service Options | | |
|---|---|---|
| Global Express Guaranteed® | $24.00 and up (documents) $36.00 and up (merchandise) | |

| | | |
|---|---|---|
| Global Express Mail® | $15.50 and up | |
| Global Priority Mail® | $4.00 and up | |
| Global Airmail® (Parcel Post) | $12.50 and up | |
| Global Economy® (Parcel Post) | $15.25 and up | |

*Days designed to be delivered depend on origin and destination.*

***www.fedex.com***

| astest | FedEx SameDay® Delivery time based on flight Availability. | | |
|---|---|---|---|
| Business Day | FedEx First Overnight® Delivery by 8 or 8:30 a.m. | FedEx Priority Overnight® Delivery by 10:30 a.m. | Fe De |
| 3 Business Days | FedEx 2Day® Delivery the second business day by 4:30 p.m. | FedEx Express Saver® Delivery the third business day by 4:30 p.m. | |
| 5 Business Days | FedEx Ground® Delivery to businesses. Delivery day based on distance to destination | FedEx home Delivery® Delivery to residences. Delivery day based on distance to destination | |

Y

pa

dig

the

and

eac

with

You

orde

are s

**Why**

- Y

- Y

- Y

- Y

- Y

  th

  w

***Good***

***follow***

*Carol D.*

# "YOUR RIGHTS"
♠♠♠
What Employers Do Not
Want You To Know

AN EMPLOYEE OR FORMER EMPLOYEE MAY FILE AN INDIVIDUAL WAGE CLAIM FOR:

- Unpaid wages (including commissions and bonuses) - Labor Code §§ 200, 201, and 202

- Wages paid by check issued with insufficient funds - Labor Code § 212

- Final paycheck not received - Labor Code §§ 201, 202, and 203

- Unused vacation hours which were not paid - Labor Code 227.3

- Unauthorized deductions from paychecks - Labor Code §§ 221 and 224

- Unpaid expenses - Labor Code § 2802

- Reinstatement and/or back wages as a result of discrimination - Labor Code § 98.7 (c)

*For a listing of the types of complaints, which can be filed with this office, contact the Public Information Unit to request a list.*

ANY EMPLOYEE, FORMER EMPLOYEE, OR GROUP OF EMPLOYEES MAY FILE A GENERAL CLAIM

## TO REPORT THE FOLLOWING:

- Failure of employer to issue written wage deduction statements - Labor Code § 226, IWC Orders

- Violations of garment manufacturing laws - Labor Code §§ 2670-2681

- Violations of child labor laws Labor Code §§ 1285-1384

- Violations of farm labor laws Labor Code §§1682-1698.7

- Failure to have workers' compensation insurance §§-Labor Code § 3700

- Violations of wage and hour laws - Labor Code §§500-558, IWC Orders

- Payment of prevailing wages on public works projects - Labor Code §§ 1775

## WHAT IS THE TIME PERIOD FOR FILING A CLAIM?

A claim based on an oral agreement must be filed within 2 years or within 4 years if based on a written agreement. A claim for unpaid overtime or minimum wages must be filed within three years. (Code of Civil Procedure § 338) Discrimination complaints must be filed within 6 months of termination or other discriminatory acts. (Labor Code § 98.7 (a) ] However, it is recommended that you file as soon as possible.

## "YOUR RIGHTS"
♠♠♠
What Employers Do Not
Want You To Know

### WHERE DO I FILE

All information should be completed on the claim form to avoid delay in the claim process. Copies of any

documents you have to support your claim should be attached to your claim form.

### WHAT HAPPENS NEXT

Once you have submitted your claim form, you will be contacted by mail and provided the name and telephone

number of the representative handling your claim. For additional information, refer to the pamphlet titled:

***"Policies and Procedures for Wage Claim Processing".***

# "YOUR RIGHTS"

## ♠♠♠

### What Employers Do Not
### You To Know

<u>DEPARTMENT OF LABOR CALIFORNIA LOCATIONS</u>

| | |
|---|---|
| **DIVISION OF LABOR STANDARDS ENFORCEMENT**<br>5555 California Avenue, Suite #200<br>Bakersfield, California 93309<br>**(661) 395-2710** | **DIVISION OF LABOR STANDARDS ENFORCEMENT**<br>464 West 4th Street, Room 348<br>San Bernardino, California 92401<br>**(909) 383-4333** |
| **DIVISION OF LABOR STANDARDS ENFORCEMENT**<br>619 Second Street, Room 109<br>Eureka, California 95501<br>**(707) 445-6613** | **DIVISION OF LABOR STANDARDS ENFORCEMENT**<br>7575 Metropolitan, Room 210<br>San Diego, California 92123<br>**(619) 220-5457** |
| **DIVISION OF LABOR STANDARDS ENFORCEMENT**<br>770 East Shaw Avenue, Suite #315<br>Fresno, California 93710<br>**(559) 244-5340** | **DIVISION OF LABOR STANDARDS ENFORCEMENT**<br>455 Golden Gate Avenue, 8th Floor<br>San Francisco, California 94102<br>**(415) 421-6272** |
| **DIVISION OF LABOR STANDARDS ENFORCEMENT**<br>300 Oceangate, 3rd Floor<br>Long Beach, California 90802<br>**(562) 590-5048** | **DIVISION OF LABOR STANDARDS ENFORCEMENT**<br>100 Paseo de San Antonio, Room 120<br>San Jose, California 95113<br>**(408) 277-1266** |
| **DIVISION OF LABOR STANDARDS ENFORCEMENT**<br>320 W. Fourth Street, Suite #450<br>Los Angeles, California 90013<br>**(213) 620-6330** | **DIVISION OF LABOR STANDARDS ENFORCEMENT**<br>28 Civic Center Plaza, Room 625<br>Santa Ana, California 92701<br>**(714) 558-4910** |
| **DIVISION OF LABOR STANDARDS ENFORCEMENT**<br>1515 Clay Street, Room 801<br>Oakland, California 94612<br>**(510) 622-3273** | **DIVISION OF LABOR STANDARDS ENFORCEMENT**<br>411 East Canon Perdido, Room 3<br>Santa Barbara, California 93101<br>**(805) 568-1222** |
| **DIVISION OF LABOR STANDARDS ENFORCEMENT**<br>2115 Civic Center Drive, #17<br>Redding, California 96001<br>**(530) 225-2655** | **DIVISION OF LABOR STANDARDS ENFORCEMENT**<br>50 "D" Street, Suite #360<br>Santa Rosa, California 95404<br>**(707) 576-2362** |
| **DIVISION OF LABOR STANDARDS ENFORCEMENT**<br>2031 Howe Avenue, Suite #100<br>Sacramento, California 95825<br>**(916) 263-1811** | **DIVISION OF LABOR STANDARDS ENFORCEMENT**<br>31 East Channel Street, Room 317<br>Stockton, California 95202<br>**(209) 948-7770** |
| **Division of Labor Standards Enforcement**<br>1870 N. Main Street, Suite #150<br>Salinas, California 93906<br>**(909) 383-4334** | **Division of Labor Standards Enforcement**<br>6150 Van Nuys Boulevard, Room #206<br>Van Nuys, California 91401<br>**(831) 443-3041** |

## SAMPLE SETTLEMENT LETTER TO THE DEPARTMENT OF LABOR

**LABOR COMMISSIONER, STATE OF CALIFORNIA**
Department of Industrial Relations
Division of Labor Standards Enforcement
455 Golden Gate Avenue - 8<sup>th</sup> Floor East


San Francisco, CA 94102
Telephone: (415) 703-5300 Fax: (415) 703-4130

Tuesday, April 26, 2_____

## SETTLEMENT AGREEMENT
Regarding Overtime Between
**Claimant**: JANE DOE
**Defendant:** CORPORATE MANAGEMENT COMPANY CORPORATION

RE:     **CASE NUMBER: 11-30777 LK - COMPLAINT**

Overtime wages for hours more than 8 (8) per day or 40 per week for the period 11/22/2004 through 12/09/2004, being 28 hours at:
$18.75 per hour = $525.00;
Plus 1 hour at $25.00 per hour = $25.00
TOTALING: $550.00

Dear Corporate Management Company & Labor Commissioner, State of California.

My name is Jane Doe. I am the Claimant in the aforementioned **CASE NO. 11-30777**. I have agreed to accept a check from Corporate Management Company Corporation for $550.00 to SETTLE MY OVERTIME WAGE DISPUTE that was filed on January 19, 2003 and was heard in your office on April 25, 2003. We have agreed to SETTLE in the full and total amount of $550.00. I agree with this settlement, which is the reason that I am writing this letter to you. Upon receipt of this payment, there are no further wage issues with Corporate Management Company Corporation.

_____          _____
**Claimant**: Jane Doe                                          DATE: APRIL 27, 2003
Signature

_____          _____
**Defendant:** Corporate Management Company Corporation          DATE: APRIL 27, 2003
Signature

## THE SAMPLE DECLARATION OF JANE DOE'S EYE WITNESS

**JANE DOE'S WITNESS**
Telephone: 510-000-0000
Telephone: 707-000-0000

## DECLARATION OF JANE DOE'S WITNESS

WITNESS of: JANE DOE,

Jane Doe,                                    DECLARATION OF JANE DOE'S
THE INJURED                                  WITNESS
Corporate Management Company

### JANE DOE'S WITNESS, Declares As Follows:

(1.) I am above the age of eighteen years old. I am not a party to this action, and if called upon to testify in open court, I would testify as follows:

(2.) I am a resident of the State of California, City of Claremont, California

(3.) I am aware that Jane Doe worked overtime on November 30, 2003. Jane Doe was new to this job, she was scared and she told me many times that she felt that she had no choice but to work overtime in order to keep her job. I saw Jane Doe working overtime. I witnessed the anxiety Ms. Doe suffered on this job because of the stress of not getting paid her overtime.

*Pursuant to the laws of the State of California and under penalty of perjury, I hereby declare that the foregoing is true and correct to the best of my memory and recollection of events as I saw them.*

_____         _____
JANE DOE'S WITNESS                            January 03, 2003

# "YOUR RIGHTS"

♠♠♠

What Employers Do Not
Want You To Know

## THE SAMPLE DEMAND LETTER

May 6, 2_____

XYZ Company
Attn: Department of Human Resources
1258 Employment Drive
Pomona, CA 91768

RE:     EMPLOYMENT DISCRIMINATION, 02/12/03 - 05/05/05

Dear Department of Human Resources:

Per our discussion, please review the attached e-mail sent to me by a witness with no interest in my case, who was also discriminated against by Guy B at XYZ Company in Pomona, CA as I was. Please review the attached letter and the initial itemization of all incidences of harassment and all expenses that were submitted to your legal department for denouement of this employment conflict.

Before going to the Department of Fair Employment & Housing, I would like to initiate a chance to settle the case with you. I believe that the full and total sum of *$10,000.00* would be an equitable and fair settlement amount for all that I have suffered, *(see attached itemized list)* and to cover outstanding medical cost as has been itemized specifically on my list. In order to cure this situation and put it all behind me I pray that we can handle this employment matter out of court. Therefore, I sincerely hope that this faxed proposal for settlement will be agreeable to XYZ Company, and to the Department of Human Resources, and your legal department. If not, I have no other choice but to have a lawyer pursue this case further.

Your expeditious reply to this ***Settlement Proposal*** is greatly appreciated. Should I not hear from you in ten (10) working business days, then I will have no choice but to pursue and implement all my legal options fully.

Sincerely,


Jane Doe
P.O. Box XXX
Pomona, CA 91768

## "YOUR RIGHTS"
♠♠♠
What Employers Do Not
Want You To Know

◘

*CHAPTER 8*
**Employee Guide to Worker's Compensation**
**Note:** *Always Reference Current Workers Compensation Law*

**You were hurt on the job. You are not sure what workers compensation is. Here is what you should do:**

FIRST:      Know that workers compensation is the insurance that the law requires your employer to have to help you when you get hurt on the job, or if you get sick because of your job.

REPORT:     As soon as you get hurt on the job, (*no matter how minor you think that the injury is* ) tell your supervisor that you have been hurt. Don't worry about how big or small the injury is report it, and the doctor appointed to treat you will diagnose your injury appropriately. If you are hurt on the job and no one is around call 911. Make sure you tell the emergency staff that your injury is a job related injury.

What happens next?

A.      Next, your employer will give you a claim form.

B.      Make sure the form is called: The Workers Compensation (**DWC 1**)

C.      When you get the form complete the "Employee" section (only)

D.      Give your completed (DWC1) form to your employer.

E.      Keep a copy of this form until you get the signed and dated copy from your employer.

F.      Make sure your injury is recorded on the 301 Form for your individual injury and make sure the manager updates all the appropriate logs.

G.      Know: The Division of Workers Compensation #**1-800-736-7401**

What are my rights?

A.      One day after you file a claim form, the law requires the employer to authorize medical treatment as required and limited by the law, until the claim is accepted or rejected.

B.      You have a limit of $10,000.00 total.

C.      If your claim is rejected, get a workers compensation attorney immediately!

How long do I have to file a claim?

A.      You should tell your employer within 30 days of the date of injury.

# "YOUR RIGHTS"
♣♣♣
## What Employers Do Not
## Want You To Know

B.    REMEMBER: you should always act quickly so as not to risk losing your benefits

because you waited too long to report your injury.

If you are injured on the job, chances are you are going to be confused by the complicated process of Workers

Compensation law. You are going to want to know what the process is. Even if your injury was a total acccident,

chances are after you get hurt on the job your relationship at work will change. One way or another it will not be the

same. Workers who are hurt are sometimes confused by the procedures.

Be sure: That you have a case and pursue your benefits fully. Look in the yellow pages for a Workers Compensation

attorney. Familiarize your-self with each detail of what your case entails:

## Temporary Disability

TD is paid at a weekly rate during the time the doctor says that the injured worker is unable to work because of the

injury. TD is paid at the rate of two-thirds (66%) of the injured employees gross earnings up to the maximum that is

set by law. The maximum rate for Temporary Disability is presently paid at the rate of $490.00 a week, *(see chart*

*on the next page for additional rates)* for injuries that have occurred on or after January 01, 1996. Wait for first

check: two-weeks.

## Permanent Disability

For workers left with any residual disability they may be entitled to receive a *permanent disability award.* These

monies are not payable until the medical condition becomes permanent and stationary, which means the physcian

has signed off on the condition as having been leveled off and will stay substantially the same in the future.

Remember: If the doctor says there has been a total recovery, there would be no permanent disability award.

Note:    *When dealing with Workers Compensation issues and or injuries, be smart. What may not hurt*

*today, may sear tomorrow. If injured on the job, always negotiate for future medical awards for*

*your injury where it is warranted.*

## Medical Consultation

When the doctor ends your treatment and says that your medical condition may be permanent and stationary or that

you can go back to work, get examined by a Qualified Medical Examiner. If you are not represented by an attorney,

the insurance Company will send you the injured party, a list of doctors, (QME) to choose from. If you, the injured

worker have a lawyer, your lawyer will choose the QME or make an agreement with the insurance Company to

utilize QME.

# "YOUR RIGHTS"
### ♠♠♠
What Employers Do Not
Want You To Know

## Settlement of the Case

When all the medical reports are submitted with a detail narrative including professional opinions by all of your treating doctors, you may be ready to settle your case. The report will be rated and a percentage of disability will be assigned to the doctors opinions in accordance with the rating guidelines of the State of California. The rating percentage is then converted into a monetary settlement amount and all ratings and preset rating guidelines are arranged in accordance with a schedule.

> <u>Note:</u>    *If you have been without an attorney before; now is the time to hire one. You will receive more of the benefits you deserve if you have an experienced lawyer to negotiate your case for you. Consult the State of California Bar Association or your yellow pages for a Workers Compensation Attorney.*

## Rehabilitation

If you are not able to return to the job you had when you got injured; you may be eligible for rehabilitation. While you are pursuing rehabilitation training you will continue to receive either temporary disability benefits or a rehabilitation maintenance allowance.

### Workers' Compensation Appeals Board

The Workers' Compensation Appeals Board is the state court for all industrial injuries involving your employer. The proceedings are administrative and there are not juries. Contact an office in your city for more information regarding your rights in Civil Court.

### Important Points to Remember

If you are hurt on the job, no matter how minor it is, report it <u>immediately</u>, and demand, to see a doctor right away. An injury or illness that takes place due to your job is a workers' compensation injury or illness. If somebody tells you, "well, you picked up that box the wrong way! Had you picked it up right, you would not have gotten hurt." Say thank you to that person, then march right over to the telephone, call the HR person, tell them that you were hurt, and tell them to please send you all forms from BC to present for your injury. If there are witnesses that saw you get hurt <u>never,</u> feel embarrassed to write that person's name down or ask them to sign a declaration, and look up at the clock and right down the time you were hurt.

# "YOUR RIGHTS"
♠♠♠
What Employers Do Not
Want You To Know

If they don't testify today because of fear, or out of losing their job; believe me, they will have to talk when you subpoena them later to come to the Worker's Compensation Appeals Board for adjudication of your claim. Honest employers recognize injuries, and they process such matters accordingly. But, remember:

"If you get hurt on the job, no matter how minor, tell somebody immediately."

Workers Compensation Attorneys are very busy. Your case is important to them. Therefore, please be considerate and keep in mind before calling about your case incessantly, see if you can handle some questions yourself first.

### WHAT YOUR WORKERS COMPENSATION ATTORNEY *MIGHT* WANT YOU TO KNOW

- I may not always be readily available

- You are not my only client

- I am at the board, a hearing or a conference OR adjudicating another case

- Your case is complicated to you; but, not to me

- You can call the insurance company yourself about your check

- You can call the insurance company yourself to change a doctor's appointment

- Call doctors (directly) to change appointment dates/times

- Do not sign anything without my advice

# "YOUR RIGHTS"
♠♠♠
What Employers Do Not
Want You To Know

## Smart Guide to knowing Worker's Compensation Maximum Benefits Rates

| For Dates of Injury on or After | 7/1/94 | 7/1/95 | 7/1/96 |
|---|---|---|---|
| Maximum Weekly Temporary Disability Payment | $406.00 | $448.00 | $490.00 |
| Maximum Weekly Permanent Disability Payment | (See Numbers Below) | | |
| 0-14% 3/4% | $140.00 | $140.00 | $140.00 |
| 15-24% 3/4% | $148.00 | $154.00 | $160.00 |
| 25-69 3/4% | $158.00 | $164.00 | $170.00 |
| 70-99 3/4/% | $168.00 | $198.00 | $230.00 |
| 100% | $406.00 | $448.00 | $490.00 |
| Maximum Weekly Vocational Rehabilitation Maintenance Allowance | $246.00 | $246.00 | $246.00 |
| Maximum Weekly Death Benefit Payment | $406.00 | $448.00 | $490.00 |

Maximum Aggregate Death Benefits paid to a totally dependent minor will be continued until the age of 18 regardless of the maximum benefit.

| | | | |
|---|---|---|---|
| Single Dependents | $115,000.00 | $115,000.00 | $125,000.00 |
| Two Dependents | $115,000.00 | $135,000.00 | $145,000.00 |
| Three or More Dependents | $150,000.00 | $150,000.00 | $160,000.00 |
| Burial expenses paid to a maximum of $5,000.00 | | | |

Note: *The information provided here is current. Laws change all of the time, so keep abreast of New Workers Compensation Laws and pay rates.*

## *Worker's Compensation News!*

Provides for $250,000 in death benefits to the estate of a deceased police officer who has no total dependents and no partial dependents for injuries occurring on or after January 1, 2003, but before January 1, 2004. **Worker's Compensation News!** Extends indefinitely the authority of a nurse practitioner or physician's assistant to provide workers' compensation medical treatment, prepare the doctor's first report and authorize up to 3 days off work if working under the supervision of a physician.

# "YOUR RIGHTS"
♠♠♠
### What Employers Do Not
### Want You To Know

AB2866 Workers' Comp requires the Department of Insurance to post on its Internet site information for each person, association or business convicted of an insurance fraud violation involving workers' compensation insurance, services, or benefits. The information is to remain posted for a period of five years from the date of conviction or until the department is notified in writing by the person that the conviction has been reversed or expunged. SB899 Workers' Comp Starting August 1, 2004, new postings and pamphlets are required for the new workers' compensation law.

### Division of Workers Compensation

| INFORMATION/ASSISTANCE OFFICERS | INFORMATION/ASSISTANCE OFFICERS |
|---|---|
| Anaheim<br>714-738-4038 | Bakersfield<br>661-395-2514 |
| **INFORMATION/ASSISTANCE OFFICERS**<br>Eureka<br>707-441-5723 | **INFORMATION/ASSISTANCE OFFICERS**<br>Fresno<br>559-445-5355 |
| **INFORMATION/ASSISTANCE OFFICERS**<br>Goleta<br>805-968-4158 | **INFORMATION/ASSISTANCE OFFICERS**<br>Grover Beach<br>805-481-3380 |
| **INFORMATION/ASSISTANCE OFFICERS**<br>Long Beach<br>562-590-5240 | **INFORMATION/ASSISTANCE OFFICERS**<br>Los Angeles<br>213-576-7389 |
| **INFORMATION/ASSISTANCE OFFICERS**<br>Oakland<br>510-622-2861<br>408-277-1277 | **INFORMATION/ASSISTANCE OFFICERS**<br>Oxnard<br>805-485-3528<br>714-558-4266 |
| **INFORMATION/ASSISTANCE OFFICERS**<br>Pomona<br>909-623-8568 | **INFORMATION/ASSISTANCE OFFICERS**<br>Redding<br>530-225-2047 |
| **INFORMATION/ASSISTANCE OFFICERS**<br>Riverside<br>909-782-4347 | **INFORMATION/ASSISTANCE OFFICERS**<br>Sacramento<br>916-263-2741 |
| **INFORMATION/ASSISTANCE OFFICERS**<br>Salinas<br>831-443-3058 | **INFORMATION/ASSISTANCE OFFICERS**<br>San Bernardino<br>909-383-4522 |
| **INFORMATION/ASSISTANCE OFFICERS**<br>San Diego<br>619-767-2082 | **INFORMATION/ASSISTANCE OFFICERS**<br>San Francisco<br>415-703-5020 |
| **INFORMATION/ASSISTANCE OFFICERS**<br>San Jose<br>408-277-1292 | **INFORMATION/ASSISTANCE OFFICERS**<br>Santa Ana<br>714-558-4597 |
| **INFORMATION/ASSISTANCE OFFICERS**<br>Santa Monica<br>310-452-1188 | **INFORMATION/ASSISTANCE OFFICERS**<br>Santa Rosa<br>707-576-2452 |
| **INFORMATION/ASSISTANCE OFFICERS**<br>Stockton<br>209-948-7980 | **INFORMATION/ASSISTANCE OFFICERS**<br>Van Nuys<br>818-901-5374 |

## KEEP IT SIMPLE RESIGNATION LETTER

May 06, 2005

To Whom It May Concern:

Per our discussion of May 5, 2005 I will resign my position as Manager of the *Hotel Maximum* on May 12, 2005. Those being said, please accept this note as my official employment resignation.

Allow me to take a moment to say thank you to Gosling Investors, and Mr. Doe Winifred, for having allowed me this great five-year career opportunity.

Sincerely,


Jane Doe
29XXX Fruit Tree Way
Concord, CA 94520

# John Doe

---

**Career Goal**

To obtain a position as Senior Electrical Engineer in the Seattle, Washington area.

**Education**

1999-2005        Clark University        Meridian, Idaho

### SENIOR ELECTRICAL ENGINEERING

- B.S., Electrical Engineering, May 2005
- A.A.S., Electrical Engineering, December, 1999
- A.A.S., Computer Technology, May 1998

**Awards Received**

Dean's List, 1999-2005
Electrical Engineering Senior of the Year, 2005
Alpha Beta Gamma Honorary Society, 1998-1999
Electronic Journeyman Award, 2004
John F. Kennedy Scholarship, 1999-2003

**Certificates**

Electronic Mechanic Journeyman Certificate
CPR, MTS and EMJ

**Languages**

English (fluent)
Italian (working knowledge)
Arabic (fluent)
Chinese (fluent)

**Profession**

2000-2005        Bloomfield Trade School        Troy, Ohio

### LEAD ELECTRICAL TECHNICIAN

- Worked as lead technician for the electrical engineering department
- Assisted instructors in the Engineering department during laboratory experiments

**Volunteer experience**

Gold Medal of honor for fund raising/"Brave Men in Iraq"

**Leadership Roles activities**

Tiger Woods Youth Foundation Leader
Fundraiser for "Black Youths in Crisis"
Pitcher for "Vons" Red Team - 3 years

# "YOUR RIGHTS"

♠♠♠

What Employers Do Not
Want You To Know

## YOUR SAMPLE JOB COVER LETTER

Make your cover letter exciting. Spell everything right and try not to go over one page. Have the letter proofread by

a reliable source. State in the letter that you plan to follow up with a phone call, but wait at least three days before

inquiring about your candidacy for the job. Read the sample cover letter before for viable input into how your cover

letter should be written.

**Important Do's and Don'ts**

Do:        Spell check your cover letter

Do:        Keep your letter short and succint

Do:        Have a reliable source proofread your letter

Do:        Mail letter in a clean envelope free of coffee stains

Do not:  Call the company prematurely to inquire about your application

Do not:  Put personal anecdotes in your letter

Do not:  Use pastel colored paper for your letter or resume

Do not:  Talk about being fired in your letter

Do not:  Call the company before three days to inquire about the job

**Jane Doe**

619 XYZ Lane
Oakland, California 94607
510-452-XXXX
Cell (510) 484-XXXX
Janedoe2@eatyahoo.com

___

January 4, 2005

**XYZ Company**
P.O. Box XYZ
San Ramon, California 94583

RE:     **Administrative Assistant Position**
        **In Discovery Lab - Job Number 66678**

Dear Department of Human Resources:

Attached, please find my resume for the *Administrative Assistant position* you advertised on your career-site today. I am seeking a versatile position chronicling the same core administrative duties that you outlined in your magnificent ad.

Upon review of my resume, you will see that attention to detail, and excellent organization are standard operations of which I have consistently demonstrated throughout my administrative career. As a manager, I worked well independently, as well as with others in a team setting. Overall, I truly believe that my professional skills match up perfect to what you are seeking in an administrative assistant. Therefore, I submit to you my resume with the hope that I will meet with you soon to further discuss my professional abilities.

Here is thanking you advance for considering me for this great employment opportunity! I will follow-up with a telephone call soon to find out the status of this great career position.

Very truly yours,

Jane Doe
JD:cm
Enclosures:   Resume (3 Pgs.)

## "YOUR RIGHTS"
♠♠♠
What Employers Do Not
Want You To Know

### More Great Resumes

In the pages ahead are some samples of great winning resumes that have really gotten people the job. When you create your resume, you are putting yourself in front of the employer to view your great experience and your masterful skills and talent. Therefore, keep the resume to one page. Use a simple layout that promotes professionalism. Look thoroughly into various job markets to select a company that you really want to work for. Be patient. Consider the totality of all your past work experiences to compile succint notes that will allow you to choose the one company that is a right fit for you professionally. Know what you want in your **_career objective_** and say it. Treat your resume like a final term paper or short novel. Research, draft, cut and paste, until the words turn out saying the wonderful ideal true things about you that you want to exemplify to your new employer. Be prepared!

⊚ Write down all of the things you are good at to organize your thoughts, checking off the things you like and the things you don't like in a workplace.

⊚ Write down all of your skills. Don't leave the obscure things you did in your earlier work life out. For instance, if you worked **_at Inland Meat Company_** when you were twelve, write it down. Just because uncle Jeff did not pay you for that work experience for two summers, does not mean that you cannot get credit for the overall work experience and your great customer service and people skills.

⊚ If you babysat your Aunt's or neighbor's kids for two summers, do not overlook the value of that work experience. You are patient, you are a problem solver and you are dependable and that adds up to experience. Use it or lose it.

⊚ Remember that the person you are applying to for the job is human. If you are a member of a special charity, say so on your resume, and or in the job interview. Your new employer will most certainly appreciate the fact that you are a giving person who uses your free time to help others. Knowing who you are helps a company to consider you more seriously for the position.

⊚ Review the sample resumes in this handbook to follow as a guide to properly prepare yourself to go out into the ever so growing competitive job market.

There will be over a million college graduates going into the job market this year. Do not let that intimidate you if you don't have a graduate degree. To get that special edge on others, apply for jobs when other's typically are not looking, like during the holiday season.

# "YOUR RIGHTS"
♠♠♠
What Employers Do Not
Want You To Know


If you have worked your whole life supporting family, your work experience will have great value in the job market.

A newly graduated college student still has to prove themselves in a new job market. If you want the job go after it.

Convince the employer of your skills and ability to do the job. Have confidence in yourself. Follow all the rules, stay focused, pinpoint where you want to go and fulfil all of your work desires!

**More tips:**

♦ Make sure your home voicemail is free of slang and inuendos

♦ Use email addresses that are professional, not personal and crazy

♦ Leave the cell phone in the car glove compartment or at home during interviews

♦ Be serious about landing the job that you put so much effort in preparing for

# "YOUR RIGHTS"
♠♠♠
What Employers Do Not
Want You To Know

## Career Objective

To secure a clerical position in a progressive job setting using strong data entry and office support skills.

## Professional Skills

- Ability to type 45 words per minute
- Basic ability to use Word and Excel
- Marketing assembling
- Data entry 6-8 thousand key strokes

- Strong customer service skills
- Strong proofreading & editing skills
- Copying and faxing documents
- Reception, multi-phone lines

## EMPLOYMENT HISTORY

**2001-2005**
Green-Tree Agency, *0512 Sansome Street, SF, CA 94104*
☐ **Administrative Assistant/Data Entry**
As an Administrative leader, I performed complicated online credit card entry into a perplexing alpha/numeric database. Administered, daily LAN backup and opened/sorted documents into batches of fifty, and then counted draft documents for the lead data entry clerk to proof and process for printing. Typed legal documents performing all duties as assigned by upper management and controlled the daily processing of all in/outgoing mail.

**2000-2001**
Plater Title Company, *0022 Battery Street, SF, CA 94111*
☐ **Proofreader**
Compared original documents against typed prelim reports, which consisted of the vesting legal description, taxes and exceptions by a title code book; made corrections for typist and prepared the prelim report(s) for the distribution clerk. Copied policies, entered timed data into Access; performed all other duties as assigned by my supervisor.

**1995-2000**
Third Brazilian Title, *10512 Spear Street, SF, CA 94103*
☐ **Alta Coordinator**
Contacted corporate IT daily for the computer system updates regarding the prelim reports status. Ordered search packages by county, received search packages by *U.S. mail*, *Federal Express* and fax. I assembled, distributed search packages to searchers by county; updated files for searchers, as well; pulled documents for the searchers by count and finished the process by performing all other administrative duties as requested by the supervisor.

**1993-1995**
Office Specialist, *3333 Sacramento Street, SF, CA 94102*
☐ **File Clerk Proofreader**
Filed title files into numerical order for title department and escrow; filed miscellaneous papers for escrow; also pulled files for recording desk, proofed *Limited Coverage Policies* for typist, entered data, assembled *LCP's* for mailing. Prepared envelopes for mailing by counties, and for lenders by name and performed all other clerical duties as directed by my supervisor.

## EDUCATION

►Chabot Community College, 1988-1990
**Associated Arts Degree, *Liberal Arts***

►Regional Occupational Program, 1991-1992
**Completion of Vocational Training, *CIS,***

## "YOUR RIGHTS"

♦♦♦

What Employers Do Not
Want You To Know

## SAMPLE ADMINISTRATIVE ASSISTANT RESUME

JANE C. DOE
6789 Work Nutshell Way
Walnut Creek, CA 94565
Telephone: 925-565-XXXX                                    janedoe2002@yahoo.com

### CAREER OBJECTIVE

To secure a professional position as a full-time *Administrative Assistant,* exemplifying strong customer service skills, excellent computer skills, and sound public relations skills, in a fast-paced professional work environment.

### PROFESSIONAL SKILLS

- Strong *Customer Service* skills
- Professional sales experience
- Superb database management; supervision of vendors/contractors

- Superb phone skills
- Excellent secretarial &MS Word skills
- Excel, Power Point, Access, Lotus Leasing & Property Management

❑ **COMPANY ABC**                                                              **2002-2005**
60411 Bread Street, Suite #200, Walnut Creek, CA 94565                *Property Manager*
DUTIES: Managed a two-hundred unit facility & professional staff including: maintenance, leasing, porter and housekeeping. Coordinated projects during major rehabilitation overhaul. Addressed resident *core* issues including eviction, unlawful detainers, and various applicable legal notices. Implemented strong prioritization, administrative skills (100%); conferred with lawyers; exhibited first-rate knowledge, specialized training, using *PowerPoint, Word, Excel, Outlook, AMSI,* mail attachments, and *Desktop Publications*; demonstrated superb mastery using Internet research methodology. Assisted in the overall management of *Presidio SRO* tenancy & staff including seven employees; contractors, and subcontractors; oversaw bids regarding upgrades (retrofitting), maintenance and renovations, expeditious maintenance control & problem resolution with strong attention to detail. Strong, effective, customer services relations with all, and other duties completed as warranted by upper management.

❑ **COMPANY DEF**                                                              **2001-2002**
195 Butter Street - Pleasant Hill, CA 94578                    *Security, Customer Service*
DUTIES: Managed front desk operations, and customer service duties; used Microsoft Word and Excel to provide clerical assistance to client staff. Created, typed, edited, all complicated reports for the client, and logged daily activities, in daily activity records. Monitored in/outgoing foot traffic, and sensitive security screens, making sure all areas inside the facility were secured. Comunicated daily with senior professionals, and security personnel, in a professional manner; won the prestigious, "Thinker's" *Customer Service Award.* From 1986/1990 provided these same services to *The University at California Berkeley* for the *Office of the President*, under James Gardner.

❑ **COMPANY GHI**                                                              **1996-2001**
195 Butter Street - Pleasant Hill, CA 94578                *Administrative, Customer Service*
DUTIES: Coordinated complicated administrative functions working alongside the Human Resource Manager, for the western regional division of *Cheese Street.com.* Lead trained managers, to 75% increase in sales. Organized and managed time sensitive projects exemplifying superb computer skills. Hired, and fired all vendors, contractors and managed the front desk, and reception area services, using 100% proficiency in Word, Access and Excel; coordinated all special events, including seasonal fund raising for local charities.

### EDUCATION

BACHELOR OF ARTS DEGREE *SOCIAL SCIENCES*, UNIVERSITY AT CALIFORNIA, LOS ANGELES, 1977
ASSOCIATED ARTS DEGREE, *LIBERAL ARTS*, LANEY COLLEGE, 1975

# "YOUR RIGHTS"

♠♠♠

What Employers Do Not
Want You To Know

## Your Sample Job Offer Letter

Mrs. Jane E. Doe
715 Greater Street - Apartment #16
San Francisco, CA 94110

May 16, 2005

Dear Ms. Doe:

This is to confirm our nuncupative conversation regarding our offer of new employment with New Starts Company (NSC). We are pleased that you have accepted the position of Assistant Manager, at the New Starts Company Headquarters, and we look forward to working with you here.

Your cash remuneration shall be $11.00 per hour, starting today. You will work (forty hours per week), full-time, Monday through Friday from 8:00 a.m. to 5:00 p.m. *(or as determined),* with one hour off each day for lunch. You will report to the New Starts Academy, located at 3456 XXOO Drive, in the Presidio of San Francisco. Your immediate supervisor will be Mr. XYX.

You will be placed on probation for an introductory period of 180 days, starting your first day of work. After 90-days of full-time employment, you will be eligible for New Start's group health insurance and 401k plan with coverage starting the first day of the month following the 90-day probationary period.

Your employment is at-will. Therefore, during the course of your employment, you are free to leave New Start's Company at any time for any reason and NSC reserves a similar right. Thus, employment with the Company is not for a specified term and is therefore at the mutual consent of the employee and the Company.

On behalf of New Starts, welcome to the position of Assistant Manager. Please sign this letter below to acknowledge your acceptance of the offer.

—    I accept this job offer

**Accepted by**: _____     Date: _____
                **Jane Doe**

—    I reject this job offer

**Rejected by**: _____     Date: _____
                **Jane Doe**

# "YOUR RIGHTS"

♠♠♠

What Employers Do Not
Want You To Know

▫

*CHAPTER 9*
## Your Personalized Microsoft Help Page

BE SLICK AND QUICK WITH MICROSOFT WORD 2002

| FUNCTION | KEYBOARD SHORTCUT |
|---|---|
| LINE SPACING | CTRL+5 |
| AUTO CORRECT CREATE | ALT+F3 |
| AUTO TEXT ENTRY, INSERT | TYPE ENTRY, THEN F3 |
| BOLD TEXT | CTRL+B |
| CAPITALIZE LETTERS | CTRL+SHIFT+A |
| CENTER TEXT/OBJECTS | CTRL+E |
| CLOSE DOCUMENT | CTRL+W |
| COPY | CTRL+C |
| CUT TEXT/DELETE | CTRL+X |
| OPEN NEW DOCUMENT | CTRL+N |
| GO TO | CTRL+G |
| FONT SIZE | CTRL+SHIFT+P |
| FORMATTING CLEAR | CTRL+SPACEBAR, CTRL+Q |
| HELP | F1 |
| HYPERLINK TO TEXT | CTRL+Z |
| HYPERLINK CREATE | ENTER OR SPACEBAR |
| INDENT, INCREASE | CTRL+M |
| ITALICIZE | CTRL+I |
| JUSTIFY PARAGRAPH | CTRL+J |
| MOVE SELECTED TEXT | CTRL+X;CTRL+V |
| OPEN DOCUMENT | CTRL+O |
| PAGE BREAK | CTRL+ENTER |
| PRINT DOCUMENT | CTRL+P |
| PRINT PREVIEW | CTRL+F2 |
| QUIT WORD | ALT+F4 |
| RIGHT ALIGN | CTRL+R |
| SAVE DOCUMENT | CTRL+S |
| SELECT DOCUMENT | CTRL+A |
| SELECT GROUP OF WORDS | CTRL+SHIFT RIGHT ARROW |
| SELECT PARAGRAPH | TRIPLE CLICK PARAGRAPH |
| SPELLING & GRAMMAR CHECK | F7 |
| SUBSCRIPT | CTRL+= |
| SUPERSCRIPT | CTRL+SHIFT+PLUS SIGN |
| SWITCH TO OPEN DOCUMENT | WINDOW 1 (NEXT TO HELP) |
| SYNONYM | SHIFT+7 |
| TAB STOPS SET | FORMAT/TABS |
| UNDERLINE | CTRL+U |
| UNDERLINE WORDS NO SPACES | CTRL+SHIFT+W |
| UNDO COMMAND/ACTION | CTRL+Z |

### FUN WITH YOUR OWN JOB BIRTH CERTIFICATE

## STATE OF CALIFORNIA

## CERTIFICATE OF VITAL RECORD

COUNTY OF _____ • REGISTRAR RECORDER/COUNTY CLERK

CRY FIRST
LAUGH SECOND
THEN HAVE FUN FILLING OUT YOUR
    "NEW JOB BIRTH CERTIFICATE"

## CERTIFICATE OF JOB BIRTH
### STATE OF CALIFORNIA-DEPARTMENT OF PUBLIC HEALTH

REGISTRATION _____ REGISTRAR'S _____
DISTRICT No          NUMBER

| THIS JOB (TYPE OF PRINT NAME) | JOB'S FIRST NAME | | MIDDLE NAME | | LAST NAME | |
|---|---|---|---|---|---|---|
| PLACE OF JOB BIRTH | SEX: NONE | SINGLE BIRTH | NO TRIPLETS | DATE OF JOB BIRTH | | |
| USUAL RESIDENCE OF MOTHER COMPANY | STATE, GOOD ... | | COUNTY, SAME AS BEFORE | CITY OR TOWN | | STREET OR RURAL ADDRESS |
| MOTHER ' OF COMPANY | MAIDEN NAME OF PARENT | | MIDDLE NAME | LAST NAME | | RACE |
| FATHER OF COMPANY | NAME FATHER FIRST NAME | | MIDDLE NAME | LAST NAME | | RACE |
| INFORMANT'S CERTIFICATION | I HEREBY CERTIFY THAT THE ABOVE STATED IS TRUE TO THE BEST OF MY KNOWLEDGE | | SIGNATURE OF : INFORMANT_____ | | DATE SIGNED BY : INFORMANT_____ | |
| ATTENDANT'S CERTIFICATION | I HEREBY CERTIFY THAT THE ABOVE STATED IS TRUE TO THE BEST OF MY KNOWLEDGE | | SIGNATURE OF : INFORMANT_____ | | ADDRESS: | |
| REGISTRAR'S CERTIFICATION | DATE UNEMPLOYMENT INSURANCE _____ | | SIGNATURE OF NEW _____ | | STATE ON WHICH NAME ADDED ON LATEST REPORT | |

THIS IS TO CERTIFY THAT THIS DOCUMENT IS A TRUE COPY OF THE OFFICIAL RECORD FILED WITH THE
REGISTRAR RECORDER-COUNTY CLERK

THIS COPY NOT VALID UNLESS PREPARED ON ENGRAVED BORDER DISPLAYING THE SEAL AND SIGNATURE OF THE
REGISTRAR RECORDER-COUNTY CLERK

## "YOUR RIGHTS"
♣♣♣
What Employers Do Not
Want You To Know

FUN WITH YOUR OWN JOB DEATH CERTIFICATE

## STATE OF CALIFORNIA

## CERTIFICATE OF VITAL RECORD

COUNTY OF _____ • REGISTRAR RECORDER/COUNTY CLERK

CRY FIRST
LAUGH SECOND
THEN HAVE FUN FILLING OUT YOUR
"NEW JOB DEATH CERTIFICATE"

---

## CERTIFICATE OF JOB DEATH
### STATE OF CALIFORNIA-DEPARTMENT OF PUBLIC HEALTH

REGISTRATION _____ REGISTRAR'S _____
DISTRICT No                        NUMBER

| THIS JOB (TYPE OF PRINT NAME) | JOB'S FIRST NAME | MIDDLE NAME | | LAST NAME | | |
|---|---|---|---|---|---|---|
| PLACE OF JOB BIRTH | SEX: NONE | SINGLE DEATH | NO TRIPLETS | DATE OF JOB DEATH | | |
| USUAL RESIDENCE OF MOTHER COMPANY | STATE, GOOD ... | COUNTY, SAME AS BEFORE | | CITY OR TOWN | | STREET OR RURAL ADDRESS |
| MOTHER ' OF COMPANY | MAIDEN NAME OF PARENT | MIDDLE NAME | | LAST NAME | | RACE |
| FATHER OF COMPANY | NAME FATHER FIRST NAME | MIDDLE NAME | | LAST NAME | | RACE |
| INFORMANT'S CERTIFICATION | I HEREBY CERTIFY THAT THE ABOVE STATED IS TRUE TO THE BEST OF MY KNOWLEDGE | SIGNATURE OF : INFORMANT_____ | | DATE SIGNED BY : INFORMANT_____ | | |
| ATTENDANT'S CERTIFICATION | I HEREBY CERTIFY THAT THE ABOVE STATED IS TRUE TO THE BEST OF MY KNOWLEDGE | SIGNATURE OF : INFORMANT_____ | | ADDRESS: | | |
| REGISTRAR'S CERTIFICATION | DATE UNEMPLOYMENT INSURANCE STARTED | SIGNATURE OF | | STATE ON WHICH NAME ADDED ON LATEST REPORT | | |

THIS IS TO CERTIFY THAT THIS DOCUMENT IS A TRUE COPY OF THE OFFICIAL RECORD FILED WITH THE REGISTRAR RECORDER-COUNTY CLERK

THIS COPY NOT VALID UNLESS PREPARED ON ENGRAVED BORDER DISPLAYING THE SEAL AND SIGNATURE OF THE REGISTRAR RECORDER-COUNTY CLERK

# "YOUR RIGHTS"
♠♠♠
### What Employers Do Not
### Want You To Know

## The Improvisation Game

### Do it right

You had a great resume and a great job interview and you got the job. Congratulations! Next, the employer ask you to do something that you don't know how to do. Before you ask your new employer how a task is done, find other ways to do it. Your friend Sara use to know how to do this task, but she has not done it in a long time and she said she forgot. What do I do? You need to know how to defend your present and future interest. Cut out the Microsoft "Cheat Sheet" in the previous chapter for quick reference. Tape it to your computer and learn shortcuts. Find the files that pertain to your specific task. Look into the file to see how it was done before and follow those directions to a tee. Never tell an employer that you simply can't or don't know how to do something that is material to your job. Companies are known to want things done in a consistent manner. Therefore, there is always tactile facts left behind by a previous worker that will help you learn how to effectively perform a task that you are not totally familiar with. If you are really stumped, visit the company web site or Intranet, or ask a knowledgeable co-worker for team player assistance. At the computer, type in the task. You will be surprised at how much help you will find. **Sample:** When you are not sure how to make a conference call or how to fill out an application right, review your guide for the professional and proper way to do it. Review the proper procedure on how to set up conference calls and be ahead of the pack. E-mail conference call participants ahead of time in case they will not be able to make the call. Tell them to email you back if they can't make a conference call. Copy their return message to all parties concerned ahead of the conference call time to alert them that a particular professional will not be able to participate in the call. Be a winner! Send a copy of your e-mail to your supervisor to let them know that you are an employee who is on top of your game!

### NOTE:

*Employment Applications No Longer need to be filed with State! One final feature of SB 1809 is the repeal of Labor Code section 431. This Labor Code previously required all employers to file a sample of their employment application(s) with the Division of Labor Standards Enforcement. No More!*

### *Don't Play, do the Application thing right.:*

You stayed up late last night at your partner's bungalow birthday party knowing that you have an important job interview tomorrow at 10:00 a.m. The application is complicated. You have been putting it off for 3 days, and now 6 hours before the interview, you don't feel like messing with it because you have a hangover.

# "YOUR RIGHTS"
♠♠♠
### What Employers Do Not
### Want You To Know

You are a good person, but you do have a life. Just jot a few things down and hope the future employer has a crystal ball to see you for the dynamite cool person that you really are. **NOT**: Never leave one line blank space in your job application no matter how great that you think you are. Review your application several times for correct spelling and date accuracy always.

If you don't have the energy to do it on your own, use your guide for the professional way to fill out a job application. Let the future employer know that you are energetic by turning in a well-completed list of your past work experience and education. Show the employer that you are earnest about getting a job with their great company. Show them that you do have the energy to complete your application with correct dates, superb spelling and attention to detail. **Remember this**: Your job application is the first impression to the employer of what kind of person that they are considering for this important job opening. *You are the right person for the job. So, act like it!!!*

# *Your Smart Guide Conference Call*
## *Whiz Cheat Sheet*

### *Your Operator Assisted 800 Number*
## 888-315-4148

## To Schedule A Call

1. Make your reservation online at www.intercall.com or by calling 1-800-374-2441. Information you need to make a reservation:
   - Your **Owner # 877XXX**
   - Your Name, Company Name, Call Leader
   - Date and time of the call
   - Approximate length of the call
   - Number of participants

2. Notify your participants
   **Operator Assisted-** Distribute 800 toll free number, date, time

## To Join the Call

Operator Assisted:

1. **At the scheduled time, dial your Permanent Toll Free number (Leader and Participants).**

2. **Operator will ask Your Name, Leader, Conference Topic and Time – Then you are connected.**

# "YOUR RIGHTS"
### ♠♠♠
What Employers Do Not
Want You To Know

## YOUR SMART GUIDE SAMPLE **E M P L O Y M E N T   A P P L I C A T I O N**

| AN EQUAL OPPORTUNITY EMPLOYER | DATE RECEIVED | FOR HUMAN RESOURCES USE ONLY | |
|---|---|---|---|
| **MAIL OR DELIVER TO:** | | Accepted | Rejected |
| **Sample Employment Application**<br>**Do it Right Company**<br>**Concord, CA 94522-7899** | | Analyst - - - - - - - - - - | Date - - - - - - - - - - - - |
| **POSITION APPLYING FOR** | | Reason - - - - - - - - - - - - - - - - - - - - - - - | |
| Print Exact Title From Job Announcement | | | |

1.    **566-XX-XXXX**          Social Security Number - for Applicant/Employee Record Control (Voluntary)

2. Name:

| Doe | Jane | None | Test Code Area |
|---|---|---|---|
| Last Name | First Name | Middle Name | ☐  1 - Central |

3. Address:

| 2315 East Pine Street | | | Concord, CA 94520 | | ☐  2 - West |
|---|---|---|---|---|---|
| No. | Street | Apt. No. | City | State/Zip Code | ☐  3 - East |

4. Phones

| 925-698-xxxx | 925-689-xxxx | 925-555-xxxx |
|---|---|---|
| Home | Business | Emergency |

5. **COMPLETE ONLY IF YOU ARE NOT A UNITED STATES CITIZEN.** Do you have permission to work in the United States from the U.S. Immigration and Naturalization Service? You will be required to submit proof of your permission to work if employed.
    *(Not Applicable)    Circle - Yes    or    No*

6. Have you ever been convicted of any offense by any civilian or military court? If yes, please note in Section 15 the date and place of each offense, the specific charge, the date and place of conviction and the fine or sentence received. You may omit traffic violations for which the only penalty imposed was a fine or less than $100.00 A criminal record is not necessarily a bar to employment. Each case is given individual consideration, based on job relatedness.
    *Circle - Yes    or    No*

7. Have you ever been discharged, forced to resign, or rejected during a probationary period from any employment within the last ten years? *Circle - Yes    or    No*
    If yes, give name and address of the employers, reason for each release and dates of employment. *NO.*

    *If answer is yes, it is not necessarily a bar to employment. Each case is given individual consideration, based on job relatedness.*

8. Are you fluent in any language other than English? If so, please specify no. *I am not fluid in any other language. Circle - Yes    or    No*

9. Veterans Points - In open examinations Smart Guide County will add 5% to your earned examination score if you pass the examination **AND** meet on of the following qualifications:
    (1)    You have served continuously on active duty for more than 180 days and received an honorable discharge by the final filling deadline for the examination; or
    (2)    You are a disabled veteran.

    To apply for points you **MUST** attach a copy of Form DD214 to this application when you apply. Written verification of disability from the Veteran's Administration is required for disabled veterans. Veteran's points do not apply to promotional examinations.
    Please check ☐ the box if you are applying for Veterans   Credit  **N/A**

| Verify (v) |
|---|
| OFFICE USE ONLY |

# "YOUR RIGHTS"

## What Employers Do Not
## Want You To Know

MY SMART GUIDE APPLICATION IS NEAT AND COMPLETE.

| Names of colleges/universities attended (Names Attended under) | Dates Attended | Course of Study//Major | Degree Awarded | Units Completed | | Type Degree | Degree Title If Completed |
|---|---|---|---|---|---|---|---|
| | | | | Semester | Quarter | | |
| A) Mount San Antonio College, t. SAC Walnut, California (Jane Doe) | 1974 - 1976 | Eng.; math; psy And Sociology Specialized in Business Management | Yes☐ NoX☐ | Four | Eight | ► | Associated Arts |
| B) Moss Lane College Oakland, CA | 1980 - 1982 | Criminal Law Eng.; Law Literature | Yes☐ NoX☐ | Two | Four | ► | Diploma Pending |
| C) Cal State Pomona Pomona, California (Jane Doe) | 1973 - 1973 | Pre -Grad Credits (5) | Yes☐ No☐ N/A | .5 Credit | N/A | ► | N/A |
| D) Property Management rofessionals of Hayward, CA (Jane Doe) | 1999 - 2000 | Property Management. Apt. Management IREM 202 Designation | YesX☐ No☐ | N/A | N/A | ► | 2000 - Certificate/Comp. |

3. __REMINDER: FILL OUT APPLICATION COMPLETELY.__ List your work experience for the past 10 years beginning with your current or most recent Experience. List each promotion separately. Use additional sheets if necessary. Voluntary non-paid experience will be accepted if job related. A resume or other supporting materials must exemplify neatness and professionalism. Documentation may be attached but it may not be used as a substitute for completing this section.

| A)        Dates 1995 - 2005 | Employer's Name and Address | Title:  Administrative/Security  (Reason For Leaving - |
|---|---|---|
| From: 1995 To:  2005 | Good Company Associates 18xx Gateway Drive, Concord, CA Salary per month $ 2,500.00 | Strong administrative assistant and security duties spanning from Bridges, Decoy Consulting and Desecrate Construction. |
| Total  Ten years (10) | | Managed duties in various support roles; performed professional security services to: KPS, First Alarm, Universal in short term |
| ADMINISTRATIVE ASSISTANT | Hourly Wage: 24 per hour Hrs. per week: 40 | corporate office buildings; did extensive writing and reporting, observations and incident contracts management. More than (8) roles of responsibility in administrative rules/policies control. |
| B)        Dates 1994 - 1995 | Employer's Name and Address | Title: Writer    (Reason For Leaving: To Secure Contracts) |
| From: 1994 To:  1995 | Self Published Writer  Home Address P.O. Box XXX Concord, CA 94521 Salary per month $ 3,000.00 | Wrote edited published grassroots book on  child abuse. performed all necessary administrative and clerical duties, typing, research duties, overall production research, public contact, |
| Total  One year (1) | | exhibited excellent customer service skills to clients professionally. Marketed finished product for quick and efficient sales. Proofed |
| PROFESSIONAL WRITER | Salary/Exempt Pay Hrs. per week 40 | approved all galleys; 100% efficiency using, *Word, Excel, Access*. Did financial/ database control,  excellent exhibition of logic. |
| D)        Dates 1984 - 1994 | Employer's Name and Address | Title: Manager    ( Reason For Leaving:  Relocated to Another |
| From; 1984 To:  1994 | University of California Berkeley:1984 21XX Addison Street, Berkeley Salary per month $ 1,100.00 | Oversaw front office and exhibited security management of Information Systems and Administrative services for the office. Made sure that all visitors signed the daily register. Monitored |
| Total  Ten years (10) | Hourly Wage: 14  per hour Hrs. per week: 40 | incoming traffic; diplomatic liaison, to the building owner. Secured bids scheduled reviews according to the project pursuits. |
| OPERATIONAL MANAGER | | Communicated effectively with clients and all staff. |

## READ CAREFULLY, INITIAL EACH PARAGRAPH AND SIGN BELOW

# "YOUR RIGHTS"
♠♠♠
What Employers Do Not
Want You To Know

®    I hereby certify that I have not knowingly withheld any information that might adversely affect my chances employment and that the answers given by me are true and correct to the best of my knowledge. I further certify I, the undersigned applicant, have personally completed this application. I understand that any omission misstatement of material fact on this application or on any document used to secure employment shall be grou for rejection of this application or for immediate discharge if I am employed, regardless of the time elapsed bef discovery.

®    I hereby authorize_____ to thoroughly investigate my references, work reco education and other matters related to my suitability for employment and, further, authorize the references I ha listed to disclose to the Company any and all letters, reports and other information related to my work reco without giving me prior notice of such disclosure. In addition, I hereby release the Company, my former employe and all other persons, corporations, partnerships and associations from any and all claims, demands or liabilit arising out of or in any way related to such investigation or disclosure.

®    I understand that nothing contained in the application, or conveyed during any interview, which may be granted, during my employment, if hired, is intended to create an employment contract between the Company and me. addition, I understand and agree that if I am employed, my employment is for no definite or determinable period a may be terminated at any time, with or without prior notice, at the option of either myself or the Company, and th no promises or representations contrary to the foregoing are binding on the Company unless made in writing a signed by me and the Company's designated representative.

®    Should a search of public records (including records documenting an arrest, indictment, conviction, civil judici action, tax lien or outstanding judgment) be conducted by internal personnel employed by the Company, I a entitled to copies of any such public records obtained by the Company unless I mark the check box. If I am not hir as a result of such information, I am entitled to a copy of any such records even though I have checked the b below.

# "YOUR RIGHTS"
♠♠♠
What Employers Do Not
Want You To Know

I waive receipt of a copy of any public record described in the paragraph above.

_____     _____
ATE:                                 **Applicant's Signature**

**IMPORTANT POINT TO REMEMBER:**

*When signing waivers on the job, read them carefully to avoid signing away important copyrights on your creative ideas.*

*If you don't agree with a particular waiver, try negotiating it out of your employment contract.*

CHAPTER 10
## Smart Job Classification

### Smart Classification

In order to move on in your career and be earnest about your future, you need to know what functions, duties and skills are expected of you in your new job. Please review the standard job classification below to make sure you are ready for your ideal job. Write down all of your work experience. Next, make a checklist of your strong skill set before creating your winning resume. Your efforts may reveal that you are qualified indeed for many different hot jobs!

### Administrative Assistant

**Functions:**

Under administrative review, the Administrative Assistant is responsible for initiating and coordinating the clerical and secretarial functions required in effective implementation of administrative policies of a major academic or administrative unit.

A designated administrator provides general administrative review of objectives.

Employees in this category are usually responsible for directing the work of clerical employees in lower classifications.

**Duties:**

1. Computer, typing and transcription as needed.

2. Establishes and implements operational procedures and fiscal policies.

3. Interprets policies and procedures as established by superiors.

4. Compiles data based on research techniques and on statistical compilations involving an understanding of operating unit programs, policies, and procedures.

5. Drafts financial, statistical, narrative, and or other reports as requested.

6. Makes conference calls; schedules and plans meetings. Hires and fires vendors.

7. Composes reports and correspondence containing precedents, which may commit a unit or superior to a policy or course of action.

8. Coordinates the activities of semiprofessional service to committees, sales and marketing.

9. Signs important contracts, correspondence, requisitions, vouchers on behalf of senior staff, and does all other duties as assigned.

**Skills:**

☐ Ability to accurately deal with difficult dictation.

☐ Ability to perform difficult typing duties, multitask.

☐ Administrative ability.

☐ Supervisory and strong communication skills.

☐ Community college graduation or equivalent in the appropriate field.

☐ Five years of clerical experience, three of which must have included supervision, organization, coordination, and performance of duties at a responsible level.

**Additional Desired Qualifications:**

University graduation in business administration.

Clerical and supervisory/administrative experience beyond minimum required.

# "YOUR RIGHTS"
♠♠♠
### What Employers Do Not
### Want You To Know

## YOUR CALIFORNIA CONSUMER RIGHTS

*You have rights* when an investigative consumer report is obtained on you. The following are some of your rights:

. Whoever obtained the report was required to give you a free copy.

. You have the right to contact the agency that made the report. You can do this in one of the following ways:

    a. You can go to the agency in person during normal business hours. You can bring someone with you. That person may be required to present identification. You may be required to sign a paper allowing the agency to discuss your file with or to show your file to this person.

    b. You may receive your file by certified mail, if you have given written notice to the agency that you want information mailed to you or to another person you want to receive the file. You will be required to provide identification when you write for your file.

    c. You may be able to discuss your file over the telephone if you have given written instructions to the agency and have provided identification.

3. You have the right to receive a copy of your file or your investigative consumer report at the agency. You may be charged up to $8.00 to obtain a copy of your report or file. However, you may receive a free copy of:

    a. Once during a twelve month period if you are unemployed and intend to seek employment within sixty (60) days or you receive public welfare assistance or you believe your file contains inaccurate information because of fraud.

    b. If you are receiving a copy from the agency relating to an investigation into the accuracy of information you have disputed or if information is put back into your file.

The agency must describe these rights to you in English and Spanish.

4. You have the rights to know the following information:

    a. The names of the persons and companies who have received a report about you in the last three (3) years. You may request their addresses and telephone numbers.

    b. Explanations of any codes or abbreviations used in your report, so you can understand the report.

5. You have the right to dispute any information in your file. You must contact the agency directly to do so. The person who ordered a report is required to give you the name and address of the agency.

# "YOUR RIGHTS"
♠♠♠
## What Employers Do Not
## Want You To Know

a. The agency has thirty (30) days from the day it receives your dispute to complete the investigation.

b. When the agency is done with the investigations, it must tell you of any changes made in the report as a result of the investigation.

c. If the investigation does not remove the information disputed by you, you have the right to place your statement of the facts in your file. The agency has people to help you write the statement. The agency may limit your statement to five hundred (500) words.

d. If information is removed or you add a statement to your file, you can request the agency to send the repo as changed, or with your statement, to anyone who received the information in the last two- (2) years.

6. You also have rights under federal law about your report. A Copy of those rights are given to you with this California statement of consumer rights. Many of these rights are also included within California law. Under federa law, your report is a consumer report, not an investigative consumer report.

# "YOUR RIGHTS"
♠♠♠
What Employers Do Not
Want You To Know

## Your Rights
## As a Temp

As a Temporary, Contingent or Contract worker, you have the same rights as permanent employees to not be discriminated against in the American workplace. Neither the agency nor the Contract Company where you work can discriminate against you because of your race, sex, religion, color, national origin, age or disability. Both the agency you work for and the company that they send you to share responsibility for making sure that you are not exposed to illegal discrimination In spite of laws that protect all workers, many temporary workers face illegal discrimination in the workplace. It is important for temporary workers to know their rights and demand the respect that they deserve on the job.

### Am I a Temporary Worker

You are a temporary employee if you are employed by a temporary employment agency and they place you at another company's work place. In this case, both the agency staff and the management staff may supervise you where they send you to work. In the scheme of things, you are contracted out to another company. You can tell by whose being in charge, the agency or the company where you work who is the boss. As a temporary worker . it is safe to assume that both the agency and the company that you are sent to are both your bosses. In order to gauge further, who is ultimately responsible for you as a temporary worker, ascertain who is supplying the fundamental tools, materials or equipment that you are going to work with. Are you working in a private business for yourself or not? How are you paid? Do you receive benefits? Since there may be many other factors that can render you to be a temporary worker, call the ERA or other organizations to find out more information about your temporary employment status.

**Remember**: If you are discriminated against as a temporary worker, the responsibility may fall on both the agency that employs you and the company they sent you to. The agency should stop the discrimination. In addition, the company they send you to may be responsible if they are supervising your work and control over you during your interim assignment. Ask yourself if the agency and the company both share or split duties.

**Remember:** If things go wrong on your assignment, you have the right to go through your agency's complaint process. Write down the complaint and complain to both companies. File a charge against the temporary agency and the place where they sent you to work with a state or federal agency.

# "YOUR RIGHTS"

### What Employers Do Not
### Want You To Know


Follow the same rules that the regular fully employed worker does when filing your state or federal claim. Talk with an employment lawyer to acquire more information on exercising your full rights. People who implement these laws as a working professional have a better understanding of how you can legally pursue your rights. Like the regular full-time employee, remember to document your case, and keep copious records and keep a paper trail of work events.

Always use the company's complaint or grievance process to resolve any problems you may experience on the job. You can call ERA"S advice and counseling line at 1-800-839-4ERA for more information regarding your temporary employee rights.

**Great Employee (help) resources to call below NOTE:** *Check the yellow pages if numbers and or locations change.*

| | | |
|---|---|---|
| **California Equal Employment** Opportunity Commission (EEOC) 901 Market Street - Suite #500 San Francisco, CA 94103 415-356-5100 | **California Department of Fair** Employment and Housing (DFEH) 30 Van Ness Ave., Suite #3000 San Francisco, CA 94102 (800) 884-1684 | **Employment Law Center** Workers' Rights Clinics East Bay, South Bay, San Francisco (415) 864-8208 |
| **La Raza Centro Legal** 474 Valencia St., Suite #295 San Francisco, CA 94103 (415) 575-3500 | **Chinese for Affirmative Action** 17 Walter U. Lum Place San Francisco, CA 94108 (415) 274-6750 (Chinese Services Available - Cantonese and Mandarin) | **NOW Legal Defense and Education** Fund 99 Hudson St., 12th Floor New York, NY 10013 (212) 925-6635 |
| **9 to 5 National Association of Working Women** 231 West Wisconsin Avenue - Suite #900 Milwaukee, WI 53203 (800) 522-0925 | | |

**Five Largest Temporary Agencies**

| | |
|---|---|
| (1.) | Adecco Employment Services Administrative support, technical and light industrial |
| (2.) | Manpower Inc. Administrative, technical, light industrial |
| (3.) | Kelly Services, Inc. Office clerical, call center, professional |
| (4) | Randstad North America Biotechnology, medical, education |
| (5) | Veritude Technical, administrative, business professionals |

# "YOUR RIGHTS"
♠♠♠
### What Employers Do Not
### Want You To Know

### **"Jean, out of the Closet"**

The rule of most agencies is, *"never walk off of your temporary assignment."* Therefore as you are reading, take heed to how Jean handled her unimaginable temporary work experience.

*Jean was a middle-aged temporary worker who was sent to what is perhaps arguably, the worst temporary assignment ever. It was the bad hair age of the 90's' and the innovative times of the dot.com computer wars. As a temporary worker it was hard to predict where Jean, at age 41 might end up on any given day. On a brisk spring morning, Jean was on her way to one of the most beautiful offices on the Embarcadero. San Francisco had bestowed her with great optimism and its awesome wonder. Jean thought she had entered heaven. Off the smooth escalator ride, Jean floated into the fine red and black checkerboard, plush carpeted area of the cool offices of the most elite-consulting firm in the city. Inside the plush sanctuary, Jean met beautiful account reps and professional people who were sat aside from the rest of the world. Ten minutes into the office, a lovely Paris Hilton type greeted Jean kindly. Then, with her porcelain left hand she swept Jean into the pine smelling, private confines of the companies most spectacular, well polished, silver and lime conference room.*

*"Have a seat," she told Jean. Jean sat on a bright red chair and Heather sat next to her in a blue one. At the long green and black marble conference room table, Heather introduced herself to be a "Senior Account Representative." From a setting center the conference room table, she offered Jean a cup of freshly brewed coffee served in an expensive black, stone-brine coffee mug bearing the Company's impressive red cobra logo.*

*"Thanks!" said Jean, as she caressed the hot cup with both hands.*

*"You're welcome Jean. I hope you don't get hot in that nice suit you are wearing," she said, referring to the expensive, black Jones of New York attire Jean had on. After sipping great coffee and giggling at Heather's cordial niceties, Jean accepted her black office key from Heather. Then the pretty "Senior Account Representative," led her temporary worker to the 2x4 confines of a narrow closet, below the basement of the conference room.*

*"This is the assignment she said. I am told by the agency that you are not claustrophobic. They said you mentioned on your application that you are able to work anywhere. So we want you to look out this peep-hole and simply write down everything you see next door." She said.*

*On the part of Jean, kindness spun into brutal aloofness, as it was important to Jean to hold back her shock of her assignment location. The dark closet was a 2x4 office, with no windows. The large peephole that had been savagely drilled into the next door neighbors wall was frightening. When Heather left, Jean cried. Soon Heather came back.*

# "YOUR RIGHTS"
♠♠♠
### What Employers Do Not
### Want You To Know

*"Oh! I forgot to tell you Jean. Do not let the competition see or hear you. We just want you to watch what comes up on Mr. Neighbor's computer screens and stuff like that." She whispered. Jean heard Heather's annoying voice, but she could not see her, because, there was no room for two people in the closet. Therefore, Heather voiced her instructions to Jean from the enclave of the shadowy hallway.*

*"Use the number two pencil with the yellow legal paper pad to write down everything you see. I am sorry it is darker down here than I care to admit. Jean, I know that you are an intelligent woman, so you know why we simply cannot use these lights. You have 30-minutes for lunch. Lock up. You will have no relief." She stated. When Heather left the deserted work area, Jean squat down onto a prickly wood plank floor to get reception on her cell telephone to call the agency. The call was dropped endlessly, before she got through. When she finally reached her agent, to verify the duties of the strange assignment, the agent listened quietly. Next, she assured Jean she could stick it out. "After all," she said, "where else are you going to find $38.00 an hour for surveying a peephole in an 8 hour day?" She asked her.*

*Later, Jean checked her voicemail to see if a real job had called. There were no messages. Coming up off the floor, she hit her head on a rough piece of 2x4 plywood that was her desk. Then she watched the neighbor play Solitaire from a red computer screen while his office mates spent the day surfing the web for mostly E-news sites. Soon Jean's neck got stiff. Later, her head fell into her chest so hard that she nearly knocked herself unconscious. The LAN system on top her head began screeching loudly in her ears. Then flying white dust mites chewed tiny holes into Jean's suit, creating a freeway to her needled skin. Suddenly, she began to itch all over. Next, a gray, powder like substance, drifted into her nose. She sneezed loud enough for the competition to turn their heads towards the secret peephole to see where the noise was coming from. Suddenly, this cat and mouse temporary assignment took on the feeling to Jean of being in a dark coal mine. Three hours into the assignment Jean's right eye was bruised from looking through the jagged peephole. Her finest suit was drenched with sweat that formed puddles into her lap. Jean had spent so much time trying to adjust to her unbearable prison, that she had not written a word. The continual screeches from the LAN above left her spinning like a top until she was completely, unable to concentrate. As she anticipated an end to this hell, Jean, the well-intended worker, simply allowed her body to slowly retreat into an abrupt, coma like sleep.*

*"Wake up!" Heather shouted. "You are the third temp to come here and fall asleep on this project. What is so hard about sitting in a room and taking notes?" She asked her. Next, she snatched the wet pad out of the clutches of Jean's numb fingers. While Jean tried to regain consciousness, Heather examined the notes: "The other's wrote something!*

# "YOUR RIGHTS"
♠♠♠
What Employers Do Not
Want You To Know

ou have not recorded a thing!" She shouted, dropping the yellow legal pad on the floor. Soon Jean was jolted out of her

rprise sleep, to find that she was dehydrated. In the meantime, Heather continued to rage over the missing notes.

was the first time in Jean's work career that she slept on the job from being mistreated and exhausted. However, she

ferred defending herself. She would save it for the judge because she knew that she was going to be fired. When Heather

cked her out of the office that evening, the next day, the agency she gave five years of her life to fired her. To Jean, it was

e best thing they could have done for her. After that experience, she was just grateful to be alive!

hen Jean appealed the company's denial of her Unemployment Insurance benefits and the firing, the administrative law

dge, for the State of California Unemployment Appeals Board, sided with the temporary worker. Therefore, Jean was given

ll of her unemployment benefits. At the appeal hearing, the smart judge tore into the agency for not moving Jean after her

all to them from the condemnable work situation.

ood for Jean! She knew her rights and she accepted her fate without drama or fanfare. She called her agency in an

ppropriate and timely manner.

She kept her cool, and now after she reads this book, she will be able to select better companies to work for!

# "YOUR RIGHTS"

♠♠♠

What Employers Do Not
Want You To Know

◻

*CHAPTER 11*

## 100 ☺ BEST COMPANIES TO WORK FOR IN AMERICA
### Note: This information is subject to change at anytime

| | | | |
|---|---|---|---|
| 1. Wegmans Food Markets | 21. David Weekley Homes | 41. Plante & Moran | 61. Principal Financial Group | 81. Mayo Clinic |
| 2. W. L. Gore | 22. TD Industries | 42. Alco Laboratories | 62. IKEA North America | 82. Price Waterhouse Coopers |
| 3. Republic Bancorp | 23. Valero Energy | 43. Symantec | 63. Marriott International | 83. Monsanto |
| 4. Genentech | 24. Network Appliance | 44. SRA International | 64. Intuit | 84. Popular |
| 5. Xilinx | 25. JM Family Enterprises | 45. Recreational Equipment, Inc. (REI) | 65. AFLAC | 85. Men's Wearhouse |
| 6. J.M. Smucker | 26. American Century Investments | 46. Kimley-Horn | 66. Procter & Gamble | 86. Texas Instruments |
| 7. S.C. Johnson & Son | 27. Cisco Systems | 47. Perkins Cole | 67. Discovery Communications | 87.CarMax |
| 8. Griffin Hospital | 28. American Cast Iron Pipe Company | 48. Memorial Health | 68. First Horizon National | 88. Nordstrom |
| 9. Alston & Bird | 29. Stew Leonard's | 49. Sterling Bank | 69.St. Luke's Episcopal Health Systems | 89. MBNA |
| 10. Vision Service Plan | 30. Whole Foods Market | 50. Synovus | 70. SEI Investments | 90. Deloitte & Touche |
| 11. Starbucks | 31. Baptist Health South Florida | 51. Four Seasons Hotels | 71. Medtronic | 91. Morrison & Forester |
| 12. Quicken Loans | 32. Arnold & Porter | 52. Guidant | 72. Vanguard Group | 92. Harley-Davidson |
| 13. Adobe Systems | 33. Amgen | 53. MITRE | 73. Eli Lilly | 93. Simmons |
| 14. CDW Corporation | 34. American Fidelity Assurance | 54. Station Casinos | 74. Emmis Communications | 94. Publix Super Markets |
| 15. Container Store | 35. Goldman Sachs | 55. Hot Topic | 75. Booz Allen Hamilton | 95. John Wiley & Sons |
| 16. SAS Institute | 36. Bronson Healthcare Group | 56. A.G. Edwards | 76. Pfizer | 96. FedEx |
| 17. Qualcomm | 37. American Express | 57. Microsoft | 77. W.M. Wrigley Jr. | 97. Roche Holdings |
| 18. Robert W. Baird | 38. Timberland | 58. General Mills | 78. Bingham McCutchen | 98. Bright Horizons Family Solutions |
| 19. QuikTrip | 39. Pella | 59. Baptist Health Care | 79. Granite Construction | 99. Sherwin-Williams |
| 20. HomeBanc Mortgage | 40. National Instruments | 60. Arbitron | 80. Ernst & Young | 100. Valassis |

*Note: Company information may have changed at the time of printing. Consult the companies website for current information, data.*

# "YOUR RIGHTS"
♠♠♠
What Employers Do Not
Want You To Know

# 28 BEST  PLACES TO WORK
## IN THE FEDERAL GOVERNMENT

| RANK | AGENCY |
|------|--------|
| 1 | NATIONAL AERONAUTICS AND SPACE ADMINISTRATION |
| 2 | NATIONAL SCIENCE FOUNDATION |
| 3 | OFFICE OF MANAGEMENT AND BUDGET |
| 4 | GENERAL SERVICES ADMINISTRATION |
| 5 | ENVIRONMENTAL PROTECTION AGENCY |
| 6 | OFFICE OF PERSONNEL MANAGEMENT |
| 7 | U.S. AIR FORCE |
| 8 | DEPARTMENT OF COMMERCE |
| 8 | DEPARTMENT OF THE INTERIOR |
| 10 | DEPARTMENT OF THE ARMY |
| 11 | DEPARTMENT OF HEALTH AND HUMAN SERVICES |
| 12 | DEPARTMENT OF THE NAVY |
| 13 | DEPARTMENT OF AGRICULTURE |
| 13 | DEPARTMENT OF TRANSPORTATION |
| 15 | DEPARTMENT OF ENERGY |
| 15 | SOCIAL SECURITY ADMINISTRATION |
| 17 | DEPARTMENT OF VETERANS AFFAIRS |
| 18 | DEPARTMENT OF LABOR |
| 19 | DEPARTMENT OF STATE |
| 20 | DEPARTMENT OF HOUSING AND URBAN DEVELOPMENT |
| 21 | DEPARTMENT OF TREASURY |
| 22 | AGENCY FOR INTERNATIONAL DEVELOPMENT |
| 23 | DEPARTMENT OF JUSTICE |
| 24 | SMALL BUSINESS ADMINISTRATION |
| 25 | U.S. MARINE CORPS |
| 26 | DEPARTMENT OF EDUCATION |
| 27 | DEFENSE AGENCIES |
| 28 | FEDERAL EMERGENCY MANAGEMENT AGENCY |

*Please note that rankings could have changed by the time of printing*

*Smart Guide Look into Jobs that are popping*
*And jobs that are not!*

| Best Jobs In America | Worst Jobs |
|---|---|
| Biology | Seaman |
| Actuary | Ironworker |
| Financial Planner | Cowboy |
| Accountant | Fisherman |
| Software Engineer | Lumberjack |
| Meteorologists | Security Guard |
| Paralegal Assistant | Non-paying job |
| Statistician | |
| Astronomer | |

| Best Working Environments | Worst Working Environments |
|---|---|
| Statistician | Taxi Driver |
| Mathematician | NFL Player |
| Computer Systems Analyst | Race Car Driver |

| | |
|---|---|
| Hospital Administrator | Fire Fighter |
| Historian | President of the USA |

| **Best Incomes** | **Worst Incomes** |
|---|---|
| NBA Player: 4,637,825 | Child Care Worker 17,077 |
| Baseball: 1,954.400 | Maid 17,077 (tie) |
| NFL: 1,836,460 | Waitress 16,083 |
| Race Car Driver: 508,569 | Catholic Priest 16,079 |
| President of U.S.A. 400,000 | Dishwasher 16,046 |

| **Least Stress** | **Most Stress** |
|---|---|
| Musical Instrument Repairer | Taxi Driver |
| Florist | Race Car Driver |
| Medical Records Technician | Senior Corporate Executive |
| Actuary | Fire Fighter |
| Forklift Operator | President of the United States |

# "YOUR RIGHTS"
♠♠♠
What Employers Do Not
Want You To Know

## *WEBS YOU MIGHT WANT TO GET CAUGHT UP IN*

AMERICA'S JOB BANK **www.ajb.dni.us**
CAREER BUILDER, **www.careerbuilder.com**
JOBBANK USA **www.jobbankusa.com**
MONSTER **www.monster.com**
CRAIGSLIST, **www.craigslist.com**

---

TIPS:   WHEN YOU VISIT A WEBSITE FOR A JOB, IT IS IMPORTANT TO FOLLOW THE INSTRUCTIONS OF A JOB
SPECIFICATION, I.E.,

♦   A JOB LISTING MAY ASK YOU TO *SPECIFY THE JOB TITLE IN YOUR EMAIL SUBJECT LINE*.

♦   TIP:MAKE SURE YOU FOLLOW _ALL_ SPECIFIC AD INSTRUCTIONS DOWN TO THE LETTER.

♦   TIP:IF THE JOB ADVERTISEMENT ASK YOU TO SEND A COVER LETTER, SALARY EXPECTATIONS AND
AVAILABILITY DATE, ALWAYS DO SO IN SPECIFIC, DETAILED ORDER AS WRITTEN BELOW:

1.   Cover letter is (first)
2.   Salary Expectations, (My most recent salary was $ _____ amount, per week, per month, per
year; however, I am flexible on the subject of future salary/benefits.)
3.   My availability would typically be two weeks; but, can also be negotiated to accommodate your
needs.

Be concise, clear and flexible in preparation for your new ideal job and always let your new employer
know about previously scheduled commitments before you begin your new job.

# The Five Star ◊ Superior You

It is not a bad ideal to prepare yourself fully for your big interview day. Rehearse your interview the night before with a friend to ensure that all of your responses to questions are accurate, and in line with the question that is being asked. Do not donate information that is not being asked of you. Play it safe. Use common sense to answer general interview questions. Bring your manners. After the interviewer questions you, politely say, "thank you." Do not babble on and on in your interview. Do not leave the impression that you are crazy or unstable and that if they hire you you might be a potential liability to the company. Stay in the middle and in job interviews always be professional. Keep in mind that you are being rated on everything from how you look to what you say, and in some cases what you don't say. After the interview, and when you get the job, stay away from office clicks. Do not gossip. Stay neutral for at least ninety days into your new job. Additionally, do your homework. Thoroughly research the company on the Web. Be prepared to know who leads as CEO, president, and particularly learn what their special accomplishments and current projects are. If you are asked to, ask sharp questions about the company and explain why you are the right person for this great job. Speak well. Be alert. Look refreshed and know how to cover up your mistakes without offending the company interviewer and making you look bad.

## Interview outer must be as follows

1.      Wear a crisp dark brown, dark blue or black outfit

2.      Be fresh! Do not party the night before your interview

3.      Get to the interview location at least one half hour before the interview

4.      Relax. Study the company mission statement before the interview

5.      Spot-check your hair. Look professional, speak well, bring your best game

6.      Make sure you present with at least two copies of your resume in a fresh binder

7.      Smile throughout the introduction and interview session

8.      Say one nice thing, i.e., "nice suit" to interviewer. Everyone likes a compliment

9.      Congratulations from me to you for getting the job

# "YOUR RIGHTS"
♠♠♠
What Employers Do Not
Want You To Know

## ou are intrinsically sharp & savvy

Answer all questions honestly, and briefly

[Point out desires for timed growth in the company

Include all relative work experience

[Keep answers relative to the posted position

Be yourself; but don't go overboard

[Use sound judgment

Prepare and present great references

[Highlight problem solving skills

If you have been fired, don't lie

[Be honest, show growth and responsibility

Turn trick questions into positive answers

[Be positive and spontaneous to all questions

# "YOUR RIGHTS"
♠♠♠
What Employers Do Not
Want You To Know

◻

*CHAPTER 12*
## Something to Remember - Employee Rights vs. Wrong in the News
### Note: Apply all new material to current year's law

Some lawyers have effectively, convinced employers that employees have but few rights when it comes to their job. Do not be bamboozled when it comes to your rights on the job. The documented cases below show that perseverance can produce great dividends for the employee who is serious about holding employers to oblige and respect their protected classes and rights under varying, specific employment law. Keep abreast of fighters who are holding employers accountable for their wrong actions and take heed to these winning stories.

### Wal-Mart Sexually Harassed Fight Back

Source: Aaron Bernstein, BusinessWeek: (2005, March 11).

Subject: Corporate America may have stumbled on a break in fighting off employment class actions. They are watching closely as Wal-Mart tries to prevail in a sexual discrimination case that will be put before the U.S. Ninth Circuit Court of Appeals. This is a class action suit that challenges an examination of how the charges could slam Wal-Mart's constitutional rights to the tune of 1.5 million former female employees.

### Backgrounds please come back on time

Source: Linda Coady, FindLaw: (2005, March 1).

A California appellate court has decided that if the employer wants to get nosy and investigate suspicious conduct on you, they have to give the goods to the employee with all the public records they dig up. The definitive statement here is: (drum roll please). "The employer must provide info to the employee *"within a reasonable time"*.

Under an issue of first impression the state's Investigative Consumer Reporting Agencies Act, Plaintiff Gene Moran was hired April 3, 2003, as a paralegal at Murtaugh, Miller, Meyer & Nelson. A computer search revealed that Moran had felony convictions. Moran was asked to resign on April 9, 2003. Moran files an employment discrimination suit in violation of the Fair Employment and Housing Act, violation of the Investigative Consumer Reporting Agencies Act, and infliction of emotional distress.

### Somebody is blowing that whistle again

Source: Associated Press, *FindLaw*

The U.S. Supreme Court will hear whistleblower retaliation case to determine whether a whistleblower prosecutor can sue his former employers for retaliation after he reported a possible wrongdoing by the sheriff's office.

# "YOUR RIGHTS"
♠♠♠
### What Employers Do Not
### Want You To Know

the scope of the First Amendment, which protects government workers from discharge if their conduct involves a "public

concern" rather than personal, job related issues relevant? Alternatively, is this case really a question of personal concern or

public concern?

he ninth U.S. Circuit Court of Appeals ruled that Ceballos' speech was constitutionally protected and the district attorney's

ffice lost this one! Will they strike out in the Supreme Court? Stay tuned.

## ow that's what I'm Talkin' About

ource: Sanchez, G. *Monterey Herald, (2005, January 28).*

ury verdict in favor of plaintiff in sexual harassment and retaliation case.

A smart Fresno jury upheld the maligned employee who said she was raped and sexually harassed by her supervisor. It took

ix weeks for the civil jury to find Harris Farms liable for the sexual harassment and retaliation against a brave female

Mexican worker who had worked in the fields for the Company for about fifteen years.

## overeignty vs. Civil Rights

ource: Kober, D. *Sacramento Bee, (2005, January 27).*

A class action lawsuit against Indian casino claims sexual harassment, age & sex discrimination, and wrongful termination.

The question of sovereignty, by the casino against the seven plaintiffs, could make this case a must see procedure. The

efendant's contention that its status as a sovereign nation nullifies them from most state and federal anti-discrimination laws

s very interesting.

## The Clock runs out for State Farm Insurance

Girion, L. (2005, January 11). *The Los Angeles Times*

When State farm cheated 2,600 claims adjusters out of overtime I will bet that the last thing they ever expected was for

employees to fight them to an end of winning a $135 million settlement. Let's suffice this case to say, "your hand-sheet can

be worth millions to you." Just keep on being the great employee that you are and keep your good old calculator very close to

your fingertips when working for rife companies like this one.

## One Janitor, three chains and a hook on wages.

Source: Greenhouse, S. (2004, December 7.). New York Times

Three immigrant janitors prove there is gold in them there mountains when supermarkets try to sell you dishonesty in wages.

Three happy janitors are now singing to the tune of $22.4 million dollars in a settlement that was reached in this class-action

wage and hour lawsuit.

*Carol D. Mitchell, CDM3publisher.com*

# "YOUR RIGHTS"
### ♠♠♠
What Employers Do Not
Want You To Know

### "Final Message to Readers"

American workers have effectively served this Country well for centuries. Consequently, we are easily led by conscience to hurry into another job before claiming that which is rightfully ours from the old Company that let us go. If a Company feels puissant enough to let you go easily; you must find your endurance to fight them and guard your good name. Your work record is life-long. So turn around, take care of your business, and preserve your work record before running into another job. Never blame yourself for being methodically and uniformly fired. Today's workforce is subjective and intractable enough for anyone to be fired or replaced at a moment's notice. I know that because it has happened to me before. As an aging working professional, I have managed three large companies. In those jobs, my duties required me to work with employees from a variety of beautiful national cultures. The most difficult thing I ever had to do on a job was let someone go, but, I was always proud to see workers stand up to large companies and to me, to defend their employment rights.

Caught up in the capitalistic goals of businesses and mergers in the free world, commerce competitiveness here and abroad bred an aggressive industry with exceptional opportunities for vast and expansive growth. However, I have watched firsthand the use for older workers diminish significantly in this Country to a point we were woefully forced out of old industry, as new and younger workers came into our jobs to handle new core concepts inside an ever-changing, complicated technological boom in the American workplace. The augmentation of computers and automation, eliminated many jobs in short notice and corporations got avaricious enough to ask for a cut of some workers hard earned benefits and to my dismay some courts granted such request. Consequently, as a growing number of American workers find themselves fired or laid off and replaced by youngsters, computers and automation, this incalculable informational handbook will make it much easier for all workers to defend their rights, and hard earned benefits in the American workplace.

When you are being fired, the process is carried out in an intricate, and well organized routine that is predicated usually on rigid boardroom demands or numbers that were crunched by people who did not visually see your great contributions to their business or industry. Corporate decisions generally are final and leave no room for job resumption for the exiting employee. Firing such workers got depressing enough for me not to want to fire people anymore. I saw fewer exiting employees who challenged these corporate decisions. I got worried. I watched helpless as many of them left behind valuable employment earnings and assets to rush responsibly and sometimes un-responsibly into another job.

Those words being said, there are still many great companies in operation that believes in their employees, and you may just be working for one of them. Constantly observe the changes in your company today and on a regular basis.

# "YOUR RIGHTS"
♠♠♠
## What Employers Do Not
## Want You To Know

s key for you to understand your *"Employment Offer Letter."* Be prepared for transition by viewing and acknowledging

real possibilities of change.

vrote this book for you, America's greatest asset! If you did not get what you deserved in your last job, use the knowledge

at you gain from this handbook to bargain next time for a better working contract. Ask an employment law attorney to

view your new or old employment contract and help you negotiate for benefits that you deserve. You are a gem. Your

ong work experience is priceless and you should get paid for your educational value and all of your work life experiences.

encourage you to protect yourself. Keep this employment informational guide at your easy dispense and utilize this manual

find out about important and meaningful aspects of how to preserve your longevity in today's American workforce and

uch more. I dedicate this book to America's working class employees. I hope that I have been able to help you understand

our work rights better. May all that this book contain assist you and yours for many years to come. Good Luck!

ere is thanking you in advance for reading this book and here is wishing you the best in all of your professional and private

ursuits in life!

incerely,

.uthor,

CAROL DENISE MITCHELL
ost Office Box 484
oncord, California 94522
CDM3Publisher.com

### THE EPILOGUE

Would you sacrifice a potential large cash settlement to ensure equal rights for all? In this case cash took a back se

to the fight for equal justice in employment in trade for justice for all. The culprit was a well known Californ

institution - the below mentioned settlement letter is one to truly be proud of since the payoff will not only benefit t

subject of discrimination in this case - *but all that will follow in her brave footsteps*. It was a case of an ill black woma

who was discriminated against by several medical doctors - who discriminated against her, wrote defamatory ema

about her and simply did not treat her fairly because of her race black, her age, 50 and her disability. The Plaintiff

this case felt it was important for the institution to face race issues and effect immediate change not only to her; bu

to everyone who would follow in her brave footsteps. When the Plaintiff demanded a non-cash settlement, he

credibility shot through the roof with the institution. She later received the requested settlement letter - dated April

2004 and she knew immediately after reading the letter that she had independently made a difference not only in he

life; but, in a lot of people's lives, black, white and other by standing up for her rights and demanding that th

famous institution do right by all others in the form of a settlement letter that she would contain forever. The letter

settlement from the *Labor Relations Coordinator* touched the Plaintiff's heart. These were her rights, she exerted he

demands, and no amount of cash would have made her prouder. The letter reads as follows:

# "YOUR RIGHTS"
♠♠♠
What Employers Do Not
Want You To Know

April 7, 2004

Nina D. Rightful
567 Earthlink Road
Detroit, Michigan  90000

## SETTLEMENT LETTER

Dear Ms. Rightful:

This is to confirm our telephone conversation of March 21, 2004. I appreciate your telephone call in which you explained your concerns regarding your experience while employed by the XYZ Company and that you wish to receive a letter, RATHER THAN MONETARY COMPENSATION from XYZ Company that speaks to the need to ensure that the laws prohibiting discrimination are being followed at XYZ.

XYZ is committed to maintaining a workforce which includes the demographic groups reflected in the general population encompassing the differences in race, ethnicity, sex, religion and the myriad of other demographic characteristics. Concomitant with that diversity is the XYZ's clearly understood responsibility to adhere to its policies and labor contracts contain nondiscrimination policies in accordance with State and Federal law. XYZ conducts workshops and training classes for the purpose of educating its population about its responsibilities to manage its operation in a nondiscriminatory manner. XYZ undertakws affirmative action for minorities and women, for person with disabilities and for specified covered veterans.

The departments where you were assigned to work *are aware of the concerns you raised*, but understand the need to be *vigilant in ensuring that XYZ Company's nondiscrimination policy obligations are followed*. XYZ will continue to work to meet its responsibilities including the fair and non discriminatory implementation of policies and procedures in compliance with applicable laws and regulations.

We very much appreciate the compliments given to Ms. Donna Madina and her efforts to assist you as well as those physicians who you reported so ably attended to your medical condition.

I wish you the best of luck in your new endeavor and again thank you for the opportunity to discuss your concerns with you.

Sincerely,

John Doe, Coordinator
Labor and Employee Relations

JD:lc

# "YOUR RIGHTS"

♣♣♣

What Employers Do Not
Want You To Know

## OFFICIAL BOOK ORDER FORM

| CAROL D. MITCHELL<br>CDM3Publisher.com<br>PO Box 484<br>Concord, CA 94522-0484<br>Telephone: 925-435-6327<br>Caroldenise2002@yahoo.com | Order Form<br>"Your Rights, What Employers Do Not Want you to Know" |
|---|---|
| *Rates reflect current price for this manual and may change.* | Because You Need to Know... |

| THE IDEAL EMPLOYEE GUIDE | RATES ARE NON-NEGOTIABLE |
|---|---|
| **Book** | **Book Prices** |
| ▶ *Your Rights, What Employers Do Not Want You to Know* | ▶ **$19.95** *(State Tax and shipping listed below)* |

| WEBSITE | EMAIL | TELEPHONE # | CELL | OTHER |
|---|---|---|---|---|
| http:www.geocities.com/carol_2003 | caroldenise2002@yahoo.com | 925-435-6327 | 925-435-6327 | Discounts/Multiple |

| ITEM (S)<br>ORDERED | CHECK<br>ITEM (S) | CDM3 ®<br>CAROL MITCHELL PUBLISHING | BOOK<br>PRICE | | TOTAL<br>PRICE, TAXES |
|---|---|---|---|---|---|
| "Your Rights,"... | # | Because you need to know.... Buy two get (1) half price | 195 | 95 | $26.69 |

| Estimated Return Times 7-10 DAYS From Date of Order | Disk/Available |
|---|---|

1. Please send me _____ One_____ Two_____ Three_____ or more_____ copies of    ▶ Price: $19.95

    *"Your Rights, What Employers Does Not Want You To Know"*    ▶ Tax: $1.74

    *(Only Cashiers Check or Money Orders accepted)*    ▶ Ship: $5.00

     Or Name

2. Please mail order to: Your Name: _____    ◀ Of Recipient

     Your address_____ City_____ State_____ Zip_____    ▶ Total Price:

     Your daytime telephone_____    ▶ Mail: $26.69

| For Other Services, (see below) : Call 925-435-6327<br>Resume ☐   Letters ☐   Reports ☐   Business Cards ☐   Tutoring ☐ | Client/Customer Signature, Agreement |
|---|---|
| Carol Denise Mitchell            925-435-6327 | |
| Mail Orders to: Carol Mitchell<br>P.O. Box 484 - Concord, California 94522-0484<br>Only Cashiers Check or Money Orders accepted | Sales Department Approval<br>Date |

Electronic copies available for $12.95 and can be emailed upon request. Email: caroldenise2002@yahoo.com

# "YOUR RIGHTS"
♠♠♠
## What Employers Do Not
## Want You To Know
### BIBLIOGRAPHY

**"50 Standard Interview Questions."** (2003, July 15.) *College Grad.Com.*
Great interview questions for employees.

**"100 Best Companies to Work for in America."** (2005, January 1.) *Great Place to Work Institute.*
Comprehensive guide to shift out right companies to work for.

**Alston Jr., R. & Taubman G.** (2005). *"*Union Discipline and Employee Rights." *Google, search*
Comprehensive resource for union members.

**Associated Press, *Findlaw.*** (2005, February 28). "High Court to address Whistle Blower suit". Article:
*"Legal Matters re: Employee Rights that is in the News." Pp. 1-2.*
Current legal decisions.

**Bernstein, A.** (2005, March 11). "California Legal Matters." Article:
*"Legal Matters re: Employee Rights that is in the News." Pp. 1-2.*
Useful inspirational information for fighters of labor rights.

**"California Consumer Rights."** (2005, February 25.) *Chamber of Commerce.*
Resource for consumers.

**Coady, L.** (2005, March 1). "Employee must get Background Check Records in Reasonable Time."
*FindLaw.* For employees who want to know background check rights.

**"Communications Workers of America vs. Beck."** (1998). *487 U.S. 735, 108 S. CT. p. 2641.*
New and relevant work issues.

**Department of Employment & Fair Housing.** (2002, November 1.) "Right-to-Sue Instructions," *DFEH - 300-03.* (2003, January 1.) Pp. 1-3.
Superb how to guide.

**EDD- Employment Development Department.** (2003, October 1.) "California Programs for the
Unemployed." Periodical: pp. 1-22. Resource for the fired, or laid-off employee, etc.

**"Employment Harassment Policy."** (2004, November 1.).
Http://www.westorangelibrary.org/harassment.html. Great policy facts for those who need to know.

**Equal Rights and Economic Opportunities for Women and Girls."** (2005, January 1.)
Http://www.equalrights.org/publications/kyr/temporary/.as Great educational tool for women.

**"FedEx Service Information, FedEx U.S. Package/Envelope Services."** (1995 - 2005). *FedEx.*
Resourceful information for times and rates.

**Hayes, G.** (2005). "My Business," *Palamedia Limited.*

**Hedding, J.** (2005, May 16.). "Best Places to Work: pp. 1-4.
Http://phoenix.about.com/cs/bestjobs/abestplaces2004.html

**Korber, D. and Magagnini.** (2005, January 27.). "Harassment Suit Targets Casino, *Sacramento Bee*
*"Legal Matters re: Employee Rights that is in the News." Pp. 1-2.*

# "YOUR RIGHTS"
♣♣♣
## What Employers Do Not
## Want You To Know
### BIBLIOGRAPHY

**"Largest Temporary Employment Agencies."** (2005, February 5.). *Boston Business Journal.*
The five largest temporary agencies in the world.

**"Microsoft Word 2002 Quick Reference Summary."** (2002.). [Computer Program] *Redmond, WA.*
*Microsoft Corporation.* Shortcut cheat sheet, (for college graduates, or every day American worker.).

**"Required Posters for the Workplace."** (2005, January 1.). *California Chamber of Commerce.*
Informational guide required postings for the American Worker.

**Sanchez, G.** (2005, January 28.). "Farm Workers Case Draws Mixed Reaction."
*"Legal Matters re: Employee Rights that is in the News." Pp. 1-2.*

**"State of California Department of Industrial Relations - Division of Labor Standards."** (2001, May 1.). *Filing a Claim.*

**Tarbell, S., Starkey, B.,** Administrative and Executive Assistant, 2^nd edition. (2002,). *LearningExpress, LLC.*

**"The 21^st Century Workplace: What Employers look for."** (2005, March 12). *University of Technology Sydney.* Great prep. Resource material.

**"United States Postal Service. Shipping Products & Services."** (1999 - 2005).
Quick reference guide for employees.

**Wagner, R.F.** (1935). "Election at Ford Motor Company River Rouge Plant, *Dearborn, Mi.* NLRB
Introduction: *"First Sixty Years."* Historical - NLRB.

**"Workers Compensation in California."** (2005, February 26.)
Http://home.earthlink.net/ssblaw/wcinfo.html Smart chart for employees.